International Perspectives on Family Violence

International Perspectives on Family Violence

Edited by
Richard J. Gelles
Claire Pedrick Cornell
University of Rhode Island

LexingtonBooks
D.C. Heath and Company
Lexington, Massachusetts
Toronto

Library of Congress Cataloging in Publication Data
Main entry under title:

International perspectives on family violence.

Includes index.
1. Family violence—Cross-cultural studies.
2. Child abuse—Cross-cultural studies. 3. Wife abuse—
Cross-cultural studies. I. Gelles, Richard J.
II. Cornell, Claire Pedrick.
HQ809.I57 1983   362.8'2   82-48524
ISBN 0-669-06199-9 Casebound
ISBN 0-669-06198-0 Paperbound

Copyright © 1983 by D.C. Heath and Company

Published simultaneously in Canada

Printed in the United States of America

International Standard Book Number: 0-669-06199-9 Casebound

International Standard Book Number: 0-669-06198-0 Paperbound

Library of Congress Catalog Card Number: 82-48524

*To the Memory of Clara Gelles and
Raymond Pedrick*

Contents

Figures and Tables

Preface and Acknowledgments

A number of forces motivated us to edit a book examining family violence from an international perspective. The first was a compelling theoretical rationale for an international, cross–cultural perspective. In the last fifteen years, the study of child abuse, spouse abuse, and family violence has matured greatly. The narrowly focused medical model, which located the source of violence and abuse within individual perpetrators, gradually gave way to social-psychological, social-situational, and other multidimensional concepts of the causes of family violence. Yet, even after a decade of intensive, sophisticated study of family violence, we have the gnawing feeling that something has been overlooked. While we may have answered many questions about family violence, and while we have built better theories, the study of family violence has suffered from too few macrosocial analyses. The work of the Dobashes and others who have studied violence toward women provides a rare macrolevel explanation of wife battering. This perspective is rare; yet violence toward women and children within families is common in many, if not most, societies. We believe that an important step toward building stronger theories that explain family violence is to consider macrosocial factors. To do this, a cross–cultural, historical perspective is absolutely essential.

A second factor that led us to assemble this book was our increased exposure to research being carried out in other countries. First we began to exchange books and articles with researchers around the world. Then, through generous invitations, we were able to travel to Europe and discuss ideas and research with colleagues. In recent years, a number of articles on family violence in countries other than the United States have been published. For the first time there is a sufficient body of literature on family violence around the world to bring together a currently comprehensive state–of–the–art volume.

Finally, there seemed to be no end to questions from colleagues and the lay public about the existence of family violence outside the United States. Our first television and radio talk shows concentrated on such questions as "How many instances of child abuse or wife abuse are there in the United States?" "Who could do such a thing?" and "What can be done?" But lately a standard question is "Do we in the United States have the world's most (or only) violent families?" As the first chapter in this book concludes, we cannot state with great confidence exactly how American families compare to those in other nations in extent and causes of violence, but we can conclude with considerable certainty that family violence did not originate in, nor is it confined to, the United States.

This book continues our personal tradition of examining family violence rather than simply child abuse or wife abuse. While enough articles exist for an entire book on international perspectives of child abuse, we persist in our belief that to understand, treat, and prevent family violence, one must realize that specific types of intrafamily violence are inextricably related. This point of view tends to generate some fairly strong objection both from those who specialize in the study of child abuse and those who study wife abuse. Both camps tend to argue that the wider focus on family violence tends to dilute efforts to come to grips with the real or fundamental problem. Such arguments may be politically valid but tend not to be scientifically substantiated.

This book represents the last product of an eight-year research project on family violence funded by the National Institute of Mental Health (MH 27557) and is part of a continuing program of research on family violence at the University of Rhode Island. Betty Jones, Roseann Kane, and Sheryl Horwitz toiled over various drafts of the manuscript and made numerous helpful suggestions and corrections. We are sincerely grateful to our editor at Lexington Books, Margaret Zusky, for her considerable patience. Margaret is single-handedly responsible for helping us move this project from an idea to a final product. Our respective spouses, Judy Gelles and Winton Cornell, were as always most understanding and helpful. Two young men, Jason and David Gelles, helped in their own special ways.

1

Introduction: An International Perspective on Family Violence

Richard J. Gelles and
Claire Pedrick Cornell

Those concerned with child abuse, wife abuse, and family violence have tended to assume that the problem is greater in the United States than in other countries. This belief, held by some social scientists and much of the general public and mass media, is rooted in a kind of reverse ethnocentrism. The last twenty years have witnessed a virtual explosion of public and scientific interest in the United States in child abuse, spouse abuse, and family violence. The amount of scientific and periodical literature on violence between intimates [42] has increased geometrically. The growth in attention to family violence has convinced researchers and much of the general public that family violence is not rare and confined to mentally ill or socially marginal families. Our awareness of violence between family members in the United States, combined with lack of awareness of family violence in other cultures, has led many people to assume that family violence, if not unique to U.S. families, is at least more common in the United States than in other societies.

The reverse-ethnocentric view of U.S. family violence is unintentionally supported by sociocultural explanations of family violence that include as central variables cultural attitudes about violence as expressive and instrumental acts. "Violence is as American as apple pie," the journalists tell us, and researchers find that powerful norms accept the use of both societal and family violence in the United States.[61]

It is no more correct, however, to assume that other countries have little or no family violence because there are no scholarly or journalistic discussions of violence in those cultures than it would be to assume that before the rise of public concern for violence in U.S. families, U.S. households were nonviolent.

Not only is the claim that families in the United States are more violent than families in other societies unsubstantiated, but the assumption that other countries are not aware of family violence is fallacious. The number of publications on family violence in other societies has been growing, and a small number of cross–cultural comparison studies on various aspects of family violence have been conducted.

This introduction reviews an extensive sample of the literature on child abuse, spouse abuse, and family violence around the world. First, we examine where the research has been conducted and what has been studied. Second, we examine the similarities and differences in definitions of abuse and family violence. The types of research methods and the theoretical models used to study family violence in other cultures are then reviewed. These sections are summarized in an analysis of what we know about family violence in other countries.

Where Research on Family Violence Has Been Conducted

Societies around the globe have begun to recognize that the family can be a potentially dangerous institution rather than the proverbial scene of love and tranquility.

The development of literature on family violence in other countries frequently parallels the development of such literature in the United States. Kempe has identified five developmental stages that countries go through in addressing the problem of child abuse. In stage one, the problem is denied; in stage two, the more sensational and lurid aspects of abuse are recognized; in stage three, physical abuse is dealt with effectively and attention is given to issues such as failure to thrive; in stage four, emotional abuse and neglect are recognized; and in stage five, sexual abuse is addressed.[28]

Perhaps the most difficult transition is from the denial stage, through the lurid stage, to better recognition and handling of physical-abuse problems. In underdeveloped and developing nations, changes in traditional ways of life, urbanization, and industrialization have led countries to identify increasing instances of physical abuse and neglect.[26,37,48,32] In countries such as Sweden, values which legitimized violence for centuries are now being questioned as these nations move out of the denial stage.[38,47,73] Even in the developed nations of Western Europe, there are such heavy taboos on the subject of violence and abuse that denial persists.[65]

We conducted an extensive study of the published—and some unpublished—literature on family violence to obtain at least a rough estimate of where research on family violence has been carried out and to learn what is known about abuse and violence in countries other than the United States. The criteria for inclusion in our literature review were as follows:

Published or unpublished research on child abuse and neglect. We attempted to locate journal articles, chapters in books, and presentations on the subjects of child abuse, wife abuse, and family violence. Articles had to be available in English to be included in our review.

Research. Our central concern was research on any aspect of family violence. Articles that discussed the incidence of the problem, factors related to abuse and violence, causes of abuse and violence, or consequences of abuse and violence were included in our review. Articles that dealt with treatment issues were included *if* they contained research data. Discursive discussions of only treatment and prevention were not included in our review.

Time Period. Published or unpublished articles available up to December, 1981, were reviewed.

Research Location. When we speak of research about a particular country, for example, Sweden, we mean that the article was about Sweden, though not necessarily written by someone from Sweden.

Child Abuse and Neglect Research

The majority of international research publications on child abuse and neglect have been studies of abuse and neglect in Great Britain. Some systematic and controlled studies in Great Britain have focused on the medical and psychological consequences of abuse.[6,34,56,57,58] Additional articles have discussed bonding failure as the cause of abuse[35] and management of child abuse and neglect cases.[60] Studies in Nigeria, Zululand and Kenya have focused on the hypothetical increase of child-abuse problems as a consequence of the disruption of traditional clan life.[11,32]

Research on neglect in Africa discusses the problems of poverty and malnutrition that inhibit the optimal development of many African children. [26,32,53] Scholars who have examined child abuse and neglect in Western Europe comment on the lack of awareness about child abuse[38,64] but also debate whether concern should be limited to victims of physical abuse or should be broadened to include all maltreated children.[27]

Spouse Abuse

There is much less written outside of the United States on spouse abuse than on child abuse. This is probably because awareness of spouse abuse has followed awareness of child abuse in the United States and other countries. No extensive literature exists on spouse abuse in countries other than the United States and Great Britain, which preceded the United States in both recognizing, and developing programs for, battered women. The majority of research on spouse abuse has been carried out in Great Britain and Canada.[7,12,14, 18,50,54]

Defining Family Violence: International Patterns

Awareness of family violence varies between societies, depending on the political, social, economic, and cultural milieu of the country. Child abuse is

Table 1-1
Publications on Family Violence by Type of Violence Studied and Country or Region Studied

	Child Abuse	Spouse Abuse
Canada	3	4
Great Britain	15	5
West Germany	1	1
Scandinavia	4	0
Other Western Europe	6	1
Japan	0	2
Israel	1	0
Australia	3	0
India	2	1
Africa	6	1
Other Third World	2	0
Scotland	1	1

recognized as a problem in Great Britain, Africa, the United States, and Western Europe, while China, Russia, Poland, and Japan claim that abuse of children is either nonexistent or rare.[64] Whether a country recognizes child abuse, wife abuse, or family violence often depends on local definitions and priorities.[10,65] While the Swedish Parliament passed an antispanking law in 1978,[73] it is reported that in many Third-World countries, children as young as six work in unsanitary conditions for up to sixteen hours per day.[53]

We encountered a wide variety of definitions, manifestations, and purported causes of family violence in the literature we examined. The enormous variation of definitions hampers definitive cross-cultural analysis of data on family violence. This section first reviews briefly the definitional problems of studying family violence in the United States, then reviews the range and pattern of definitions of child abuse and spouse abuse found in the international literature.

Defining Abuse and Violence

A central problem of research on family violence in the United States is the range and diversity of definitions of child abuse, spouse abuse, and violence. The terms *abuse* and *violence* are not conceptually equivalent. In some instances, abuse refers to a subset of violent behavior: that which results in injury to the victim. An example is the definition of Kempe et al.[29] of child abuse as a clinical condition (that is, with diagnosable medical and physical symptoms) of those who had been deliberately injured by physical assault. The definition of Straus et al.[61] of child and wife abuse referred only to those acts of violence that had a high probability of causing injury to the victim.

Other definitions of child and wife abuse refer to mistreatment, including, but extending far beyond, acts of injurious violence. Malnourishment, failure to thrive, sexual abuse, and medical neglect are nonviolent phenomena included in many definitions of child abuse.[20] Some definitions of wife abuse include nonviolent acts, such as nonviolent sexual abuse, but the central definitional problem with wife abuse is specifying acts of physical violence which are considered abusive.

In short, while definitions of violence can include *all* forms of physical aggression, definitions of abuse range from injurious physical aggression to a wide gamut of nonphysical maltreatment. Other dilemmas in defining abuse and violence concern acts of commission versus acts of omission (is abuse only an act of commission?); intent versus nonintent (is abuse only an intentional act?); and whether abuse and violence are acts committed by individuals or institutions.

International Definitions of Child Abuse

There is little consensus about definitions of child abuse among investigators studying the problem around the world (as little, in fact, as is found in the United States). We did, however, find some patterns, especially when we examined definitions used in studies within one country or world region. Our analysis of child-abuse definitions focused on three aspects of the definitions: first, the range of behaviors considered abusive; second, whether an abusive act had to be intentional; and third, the level of analysis of the definitions (individual, organizational, or societal/institutional).

Great Britain. Of the materials we reviewed, the majority of published research on child abuse was from Great Britain. These studies focused on physical abuse.[2,23,25,34,40,46,52,56,57,58] But, as would be expected in this area of study, some investigators did examine the broader manifestations of abuse, including neglect[6,60] and children at risk.[35,51]

An examination of the literature on abuse in Great Britain reveals disagreement about whether abuse is limited to intentional acts or whether intent is relevant at all to a definition of abuse. Approximately half of the publications on abuse explicitly state or imply that intentionality is a necessary component of a definition of child abuse, while the other half do not specify intent as a part of the definition. Nearly all of the reports that do not specify intent as a component of a definition of abuse are medical studies focusing on the physical outcomes of child abuse.

All the definitions of child maltreatment in the literature on child abuse in Great Britain viewed child abuse as acts of violence or mistreatment committed by one individual against a child. None of the studies examined or even defined abuse as acts committed by organizations (for example, police, medical, group homes) or societal institutions (for example, social policies which are harmful to children).

European Countries. Kamerman[27] reports that definitions of child abuse vary from one European country to the next, depending upon the cultural perceptions of children and the *perceived* extent of child abuse in the respective countries. We also find inconsistent definitions of abuse from the research reports on child maltreatment in Italy, France, West Germany, Poland, and Yugoslavia.

Most of the reports fail to distinguish between acts of physical abuse and acts of neglect. Although investigators who examined child abuse in France and Germany provide loose definitions of abuse, they appear to be undecided about whether abuse should be addressed as a conceptually distinct issue or whether the main focus of concern should be on all victimized children, regardless of the form of maltreatment.[27]

The research reports a variation in societal concern for child abuse in European countries. Poland apparently recognizes the existence of child abuse but does not regard it as a serious problem.[27] Yugoslavia and Italy appear to be minimally concerned with the issue of child abuse,[27] and Yugoslavia does not even distinguish abuse from the general issue of predelinquency.

The issue of intent is not discussed at all by those writing on abuse in European countries, in contrast to British writers' partial concern with this aspect of the definition.

Another example of contrast with Great Britain is that most studies on abuse in Europe view abuse as a consequence of societal policies that sanction or lead to less than optimal child development compared with a focus on the individual in British analyses of child abuse. For example, in Maroulis's study[38] in Greece, abuse is seen as a condition caused by societal change, while the study by Tauber et al.[64] in Italy traces the causes of abuse to society's lack of social awareness of the problem.

Scandinavia. Child abuse is not generally seen as an overwhelming problem in Scandinavian countries for several reasons: first, social conditions are good; second, there is widespread use of contraceptives and free abortions, reducing the number of unwanted babies; third, many mothers work and leave their babies in day-care institutions; and last, premature babies are kept in a neonatal ward until they are a certain weight and are released only when their parents are taught how to handle the newborn.[71] Perhaps the perceived lack of a problem contributes to the lack of consensus regarding a definition of child abuse in Norway, Denmark, Sweden, and The Netherlands. The various definitions include acts of wilful abuse, emotional deprivation,[63] as well as spanking and humiliation of children.[73]

Reports on abuse in Scandinavian countries discuss intent but differ about whether it is an important part of a definition of abuse. A slight majority of the reports look at abuse from the societal/institutional level of analysis. There was also one report on organizational abuse of children (the result of "studied nonobservance" among medical professionals.[63]

Australia and Canada. There were too few studies of child abuse in Canada or Australia to allow meaningful comparisons of the definitions of child abuse used by researchers in these countries. Researchers in Australia did discuss intent but did not agree on its importance. Studies of abuse in these countries followed Great Britain's pattern of focusing only on the individual, caretaker-to-child, level of analysis.[44,45]

There was no consensus among those studying abuse in Canada about either a definition of child maltreatment or the issue of intent. Kamerman[27] reports that Canada and Great Britain are the two countries that follow the precedent established in the United States of distinguishing acts of abuse from acts of neglect.

Research in Canada has examined issues such as sexual abuse[13] and the mass media as an agent of abuse that perpetuates and encourages violence between intimates.[3]

Third-World Nations. Researchers studying abuse in Third-World countries used the broadest definitions of child abuse. A unique aspect of their definitions of child abuse is the use of the societal/institutional level of analysis. Concerns of Third-World investigators included "nutritionally battered" children,[4,26] a form of abuse ignored by studies of abuse in all other areas of the world. Abuse was also defined more broadly in the Third World than in other regions of the world. A major concern in Third-World definitions of abuse is impaired development of children or even death resulting from *any* adverse environmental factors that could have been prevented by way of scientific knowledge or adequate health services.[4]

Finally, the majority of definitions did not consider the issue of intent.

In summary, the problems of definitional variation and the resulting incomparability of research based on the various definitions—which have long plagued investigators in the United States—are evident in worldwide concern about child abuse. We found some definitional consistency within specific countries or regions; however, the definitional problems found in research in the United States are amplified when cross-cultural variations in attitudes toward violence and children influence definitions of abuse. Those interested in theories of abuse will be stymied by explanations that focus on widely varying phenomena.

Definitions of Spouse Abuse

In countries other than the United States, there have been fewer reports on spouse abuse than on child abuse. This discrepancy between the number of articles on spouse abuse and on child abuse could be an international reflection of the trend in the United States, where child abuse was identified as a significant social and family problem ten years before spouse abuse was.[17]

Spouse abuse is almost uniformly viewed as wife abuse in the worldwide as well as U.S. literature.[5,7,8,12,14,21,24,33,36,41,54,68] The definitions of wife abuse are much more consistent than those of child abuse. While the child-abuse literature is full of controversies over issues such as abuse, neglect, failure to thrive, being "at risk" and intent, the spouse-abuse literature is in overwhelming agreement that spouse abuse is physical abuse, with the intent of one spouse to injure or cause harm to the other.

Although there is much agreement on definitions in the spouse-abuse literature, there is also some difference among researchers about the severity necessary for an act to be defined as abusive, and about whether spouse abuse occurs on the individual, organizational, or societal level.

Great Britain. Researchers in Great Britain agree that physical violence is the primary factor in determining if a person is a victim of spousal violence. However definitions of physical abuse vary from "deliberate, severe and repeated demonstratable [*sic*] physical injury from the husband" [14,21] to physical abuse and malign intent, both defined as "cruelty" by English divorce laws.[8] The majority of researchers believe that spouse abuse occurs on individual, organizational, and societal levels.[5,8,12,21] Studies focusing on the individual level of analysis examine the characteristics of the abused, abuser, or abusive situation.[5,8,12,14,21] Gregory[21] has discussed the problems faced by battered women because of organizational constraints imposed upon them from the law, police, inadequate housing, and financial difficulties. All of these factors work against abused women and force them to remain in abusive situations. Finally, researchers interpret the existence and continuance of domestic violence as a result of societal attitudes and institutions that allow men to abuse their wives.[5,10,12,21] These attitudes support the idea of the *sanctity of marriage*, which insulates family violence from public awareness.

Canada. In Canada, researchers agree that spouse abuse means physical violence with intent to injure. Abusive acts include actual or threatened abuse;[7] slapping, pushing, and punching;[54] deliberate, severe and repeated abuse; [69] and murder.[54] As in Great Britain, researchers examine spouse abuse from the individual, organizational, and societal levels of analysis. Gerson [18] and Van Stolk[69] investigate abuse between spouses on the individual level by analyzing the role of alcohol[18] and pregnancy[69] in precipitating violence. Byles[7] delves into the organizational role of police in uncovering and responding to cases of domestic disturbances, and Schlessinger[54] and Van Stolk[69] focus on the history of male dominance that has granted men the right and duty to beat women. The definition and level of analysis used in Canada is very similar to that in Great Britain.

Other European Countries. Researchers in Germany, Portugal, Sicily, Greece, and Cyprus define spouse abuse as physical abuse with either intent to injure[24] or as necessary to maintain the moral code of the society.[33] Unfortunately, the researchers failed to provide concise definitions of acts constituting abuse, beyond such terms as *wife abuse* or *wife beating.* Abuse against women is viewed as existing on the societal level because of cultural attitudes that grant men permission to use aggressive force against their wives. [24,33] In Mediterranean countries, the use of violence by husbands toward their wives and children is considered necessary and proper to preserve the family's integrity.

In summary, spouse abuse is vaguely defined as physical abuse with intent to injure or control. Abuse is examined primarily from the societal level of analysis. In many countries violence against women by their husbands is perceived as being virtually sanctioned by the societal taboo against public awareness of such violence.[24]

Japan and India. Researchers of spousal violence in Japan and India[30,31] place equal emphasis on physical abuse and verbal abuse in resolving family conflict. Researchers report lower rates of spousal violence in Japan and India than in the United States, and explain this in terms of the differences in the cultural context of the two countries. The dominant cultural context in Japan is a traditional and reserved way of life, with emphasis placed on male supremacy and traditional sex–role identification.

India, characteristically a nonviolent society, places great emphasis on the traditional, subordinate role of women.

The higher rates of conjugal violence in the United States are explained as characteristics of the more expressive American culture, with its movement toward equal rights between the sexes.[30]

Africa. Researchers of spouse abuse in Africa[41] have investigated varying rates of victimization of women and of female homicide, in a variety of tribes throughout East and Central Africa. The exact definition of *victimization* was not disclosed and so we can only guess at the types of behavior included in such a vague description. Abuse in Africa is seen as occurring on the societal level because of the cultural values that legitimize spouse abuse as a way of resolving conflict.[41]

In summary, researchers in England and Canada use a broad definition of spouse abuse, ranging from actual to threatened acts of violence. These acts vary in severity from slaps to murder, and victimization is believed to occur on all levels of society. Japan and India fall in the middle of the definitional continuum. Although the researchers take into consideration both verbal and physical abuse between spouses, they define abuse as occurring on the societal level because of the varying cultural context of each country. African cultures and European countries use the narrowest definition of spouse abuse. It was impossible to determine the range of acts that constituted abusive behavior. In both regions, abuse is examined from the societal level, focusing on prevalent attitudes that allow and even encourage husbands to abuse their wives.

Methodological and Theoretical Approaches

Methods

Child Abuse. Researchers have used five approaches to gathering and presenting data on child abuse in other countries: position papers, survey research, case–control designs, clinical case studies, and literature reviews.

The position paper is the most commonly used approach for discussing child abuse. Position papers purport to give current or historical accounts of the causes of child abuse in various countries. It is debatable whether this technique is an acceptable scientific approach, since many of the researchers who use this technique draw conclusions based upon accounts of societal events without using either empirical evidence or developed social theory to substantiate their conclusions. The position paper is usually lacking in hard data and is essentially based on the researcher's non-systematic observations of social conditions that might lead to the abuse of children.[3,22,26,32,37, 38,47,48,53,64] Position papers are the most frequent form for discussing child abuse in Third-World countries[26,32,37,47,48] and also are used (though with much less frequency) in Canada,[3] Scandinavia,[73] Greece, [38] and Italy.[64] Authors of position papers primarily describe what they see as causes of child abuse. Among the purported causes are the mass media's visual depiction of family violence[3], recent urbanization and industrialization trends in developing countries,[26,32,37,38,48] and attempts to break the cycle of violence by prohibiting the use of any form of physical punishment—even spanking—by parents against their children.[73]

Survey research is the second most widely used approach to child abuse. Survey designs are used by researchers in a variety of countries, including Great Britain,[6,46,51,60] African countries,[11] Scandinavian countries, [67] Australia,[44] and Scotland.[49] With the exceptions of the review by Christoffel et al.[9] of fifty-two countries and their rates of childhood homicide, and Kamerman's[27] cross–cultural study of perspectives on child abuse and neglect, researchers have drawn their samples from a single country and typically a single medical institution in the country. The limits of such sampling techniques—that is, drawing the sample from cases of abuse seen in either a hospital or therapeutic institution—call into question whether the sample is representative of the problem of abuse. No evidence is provided in any of the studies that the institution selected or cases of abuse examined are representative of other medical institutions or cases of abuse in the country.

Case–control designs rank third among modes of research used to examine abuse in other countries. This design, while not using random assignment or manipulation of the independent variable, does use natural experimental and control groups. In this type of research the experimental groups consist of children officially identified as victims of abuse, while the control groups are children (sometimes matched on such characteristics as age, race, and sex) who have not been publicly identified as abused. Case–control designs are used primarily in Great Britain,[25,34,35,56,57,58] although researchers in Australia[45] and Africa[68] have also used this design.

Researchers have used case–control designs to examine the causes of child abuse. By using control groups, they hope to discover whether a particular variable (for example, stress) is significantly more common in abusive than in nonabusive families.[25,35,45,56,57,58] Case–control designs have also been used in follow–up studies of abused children.[34,68] Follow–up studies investigate victims of child abuse years after the abusive incident to monitor mental and physical development (compared to nonabused children).

Clinical case studies present detailed descriptions of specific incidents of child abuse. These descriptions are predominantly medical ones and provide information on the abused, abuser, and abusive situation.[4,23,40,46,52,63] Clinical case studies are usually based on very small numbers of cases, which severely restricts their generalizability. The case studies we reviewed had sample sizes ranging from one[40] to twenty-three cases.[23] Researchers from Great Britain,[23,40,46,52] India,[4] and Scandinavia[63] have used this design.

Researchers have used clinical case studies as a means of helping physicians become more aware of types of child abuse, including poisoning,[52] suffocation,[40] or shaking a child severely enough to cause subdural hematoma.[46]

Bhattacharyya[4] uses thirteen cases to arrive at the causes of child abuse. Although he concludes that urbanization, the breakdown of the extended family, and increasing numbers of women entering the work force contribute to abuse of children in India, his data do not really provide the information necessary to draw such conclusions. Tangen[63] uses clinical investigations to demonstrate the mismanagement of twelve cases of child abuse by doctors who did not recognize abuse as the life threatening situation that it is.

A few articles on child abuse are reviews of the child-abuse literature in particular countries, as opposed to analyses of primary data. Researchers in England,[2] Canada,[13] Scandinavia,[71] and France[62] have used this method to provide a more comprehensive picture of the incidence rates,[62, 71] treatment,[2,62] and psychological damage abuse victims have incurred. [62] Gammon[13] carefully criticizes the currently available research by noting definitional inconsistency regarding abuse and neglect. She also analyzes the variety of theoretical approaches taken, and ends by providing her own interaction model of child abuse.

Spouse Abuse. Literature reviews are the dominant approach to the study of spouse abuse around the world.[5,12,21,36,41,54] Researchers in Great Britain,[5,12,21] Canada,[54] and Africa[41] have primarily reviewed incidence statistics. Unfortunately, the researchers have not been able to provide valid or reliable data on the number of women who are abused each year. The statistics are typically confined to reports of rates of homicide[36,41] or they are projections from a very select population of female assault victims.[12,21, 54] Researchers have also reviewed the causes of spouse abuse,[5,21,36,41] the management of cases of abuse by police and the courts,[21,54] and have given detailed descriptions of the typical abuse victim.[21]

The second most popular design for studying spouse abuse, survey research, has been used in Great Britain[8,14] and Canada.[7,18,69] Survey researchers examine the causes of spouse abuse[14,18,69] and the management of cases by the police and courts.[7,8] Gayford[18] and Byles[7] also provide detailed descriptions of the forms, patterns, and likelihood of abuse. It should be noted, however, that *all of the researchers* have relied on samples of women who have been publicly recognized as victims by either the police, courts, or by women's shelters. Research on child and spouse abuse in the United States has clearly demonstrated that those cases that come to public attention represent a skewed portion of the population of abuse victims.[16, 61] Research in the United States has also shown that social, racial, and economic factors influence who becomes labeled as abused.[43,66]

Among the more sophisticated surveys of abuse in other countries are the studies of conflict resolution between spouses in Japan, India, and the United States.[30,31] These surveys were among the few to employ comparison groups and cross-cultural designs. The investigators studied high-school seniors from the three countries and asked them to report on rates of verbal and physical violence between their parents. Also studied were the factors related to violent behavior. The data on spouse abuse from these surveys support Taylor and Newberger's[65] claim that rates of child abuse are lower in Japan than in the United States.

Position papers are much less common in the spouse-abuse literature than the child-abuse literature. Haffner[24] describes the birth of the movement to build shelters for battered women in Germany, while Loizos[33] describes the historical significance of the *moral code* in perpetuating family violence in Mediterranean countries. Loizos postulates the causes of abuse, while Haffner[24] reports on the incidence and management of cases of spouse abuse. Haffner also discusses the lack of awareness of spouse abuse. Although neither article contains hard scientific evidence, both provide us with glimpses into the impact of cultural values on spouse abuse.

We found no examples of either case–control designs or clinical case studies in the literature on spouse abuse. Brandon[5] does note that the data he presents are based on some of his own clinical observations, but he does not report the number or nature of the observations.

In summary, a variety of methods of data collection and analysis have been used by students of both child abuse and spouse abuse in countries around the world. These methods are, by and large, similar to methods used to study these issues in the United States, and thus the problems with the methods and conclusions are also similar. The studies of family violence in other countries have a variety of limitations which are similar to those found in research in the United States. The limitations include: failure to use comparison groups in surveys; small nonrepresentative samples; samples frequently based only on officially recognized cases of abuse; samples drawn from a single source (such as a hospital, shelter, institution); and conclusions that are often post hoc, or without empirical or theoretical support.

Theories

Child Abuse. During the early years of research, theoretical approaches to child abuse in the United States were characterized largely by medical and intraindividual models. Gradually, these models gave way to broader approaches which emphasized social–psychological variables.[15] Although some noted students of abuse have approached the problem from a sociocultural level of analysis,[19] theoretical models that attempt to explain child abuse in the United States using macrolevel variables have been rare.

In contrast to theoretical approaches in the United States, the most widely applied model we found in the worldwide child-abuse literature was a *sociostructural* model. An approach emphasizing social structures, norms, values, and institutional arrangements has been the dominant theoretical approach used by researchers in Africa and India.[4,11,32,37,38,47,48,53] Researchers studying and attempting to explain abuse in developing nations have drawn on a social-disorganization approach, which sees abuse as rising from changes in traditional tribal ways of life. Researchers who apply the sociocultural model to developed nations have focused on the changing demands placed on the family by society and the role of the media in creating unreasonable demands on the family.[67] The cultural legitimization of family violence has also been proposed as a significant explanatory factor.[3] Previously we cited Vesterdal's[71] proposition that low rates of child abuse in Denmark were due to good social conditions.

The second most widely used theoretical approach to child abuse world-wide has been the social–psychological model of maltreatment. Here researchers have located the source of abuse primarily in mother–child interactions, resulting from failures to bond,[35] abnormalities in newborns (such as low birth weights, prematurity, or congenital defects),[45,58] and other inappropriate mother–child interactions.[22,25] (disjointed or unreciprocated interaction, unrealistic expectations or overreactions to problems) Others have discussed abuse rising out of parental discord or domestic upheaval.[44, 46,52] Violence toward children is also seen as rising from parental backgrounds that include violence, broken homes, and poverty.[26,38] These social–psychological theories have been applied in England,[25,35,46,52,58] Africa,[26] Canada,[13] Australia,[22,44,45] and Greece.[38]

Medical and intraindividual models locate the causes of abuse within the individual (for example, alcohol, psychopathy, sociopathy, mental illness). Authors who approach abuse using a medical model often aim at goals other than explaining abuse. Some have used this model to sensitize other physicians to the possibility of abuse in cases of poisoning, suffocation, submersion, and subdural hematoma resulting from severe shaking.[23,40,44,46,52] Others have used the model to assess the mental development of children after incidents of abuse.[6,68]

The medical model is most widely used by investigators of abuse in Great Britain.[2,6,23,40,46,52] It is also used in studies of abuse in Africa,[68] Australia,[44] and Scotland.[49]

Spouse Abuse. Students of spouse abuse, both in the United States and around the world, have approached the subject primarily from a social–psychological perspective. Social learning theory has been widely applied in the United States, Canada, and Great Britain.[14,21,54] Kumagai[30] has used field theory to study spousal violence in Japan, and has tested catharsis theory with Straus in studies of spousal violence in three countries.[31] Differential-association theory, as adapted from theories of deviance, has been tested,[41] and researchers have also considered the impact of marital communication and pregnancy in cases of spousal abuse.[5,69] Social-psychological models have been used in both developing and developed countries.

Researchers have also located the causes of spouse abuse in social-structural and cultural variables. There is a strong tradition in studies of wife abuse to trace the primary generative sources of abuse to cultural attitudes and assumptions that support and legitimize the use of violence toward women.[5, 10,21,33,36] While investigators in the United States have also focused on cultural attitudes and patriarchy as causes of abuse, this theory has an even stronger tradition in Great Britain and Mediterranean countries.[33]

Only two of the earliest publications on spouse abuse in the United States employed a medical–psychopathological model.[55,59] We found no spouse abuse studies in the worldwide literature that used a medical model. A few investigators, however, located the sources of abuse in drugs and alcohol.[5, 18] These investigators used the traditional argument that alcohol and drugs serve as disinhibitors which break down the restraints against violent behavior.

In summary, there appears to be a much wider application of social-structural models of family violence to the issues of child and spouse abuse in countries around the world than in research in the United States. This could be because research on child and spouse abuse in other countries began after intraindividual models had fallen into disrepute in the United States. However, another plausible explanation is that the dominant paradigm used by researchers in Europe and Third-World countries for studying social problems such as family violence does not attempt to locate the problem in bad people but rather in social relations or social structures.

What We Know About Family Violence in Other Countries

As noted earlier, what we know about the nature, extent, patterns, causes, and other aspects of family violence around the world largely depends on the degree to which specific societies recognize the existence of family violence or define it as problematic and deviant. As norms and attitudes vary, so do the research efforts, data collection mechanisms, and thus the knowledge generated about family violence.

Existence and Extent

Child Abuse. Much of the early knowledge about the existence and extent of child abuse in the United States came as a result of the federal government urging the states to pass mandatory reporting laws. These laws, enacted in all fifty states by the end of the 1960s, not only allowed for estimates of extent of abuse, but provided potential pools of subjects for research into the patterns, causes, and consequences of child abuse. Kamerman,[27] in her cross-cultural review of social-service systems in eight countries, found no firm data on the incidence of child abuse in the countries she examined. Moreover, only the United States and Canada had specific legislation dealing with child abuse and programs developed to identify abuse. Canada, France, West Germany, Israel, Poland, the United Kingdom, and the United States had legislation on child neglect.

Our review of the literature on child abuse in other countries found considerably less concern for estimating the incidence of abuse than there has been in the United States. Even before there were mandatory reporting statutes and incidence studies, researchers in the United States tried to estimate how large the problem of abuse was. We found only one example of incidence-estimates in a discussion of abuse which applied Kempe's U.S. incidence-estimates to Italy, and concluded that one could expect three thousand or four thousand cases of abuse per year in Italy.[64]

Investigators have reported that child abuse and violence toward children is most common in developed countries.[9,65] Violence and abuse are considered rare in developing nations,[9,11] Denmark,[72] China, Russia, Poland, Japan, and Italy.[65]

While estimates of the incidence of abuse are rare, a number of researchers have voiced their concern that social change, urbanization, industrialization, and population growth have led to a breakdown in traditional cultural values and family structure, which has caused an increase in the problem of abuse and neglect.[4,26,32,38,48] These concerns are strongest in developing nations and Third-World countries.

Spouse Abuse. As in the United States, few countries actually record data on wife beating. Some incidence estimates have been made for Great Britain. Gregory[21] cites Marsden and Owens's[39] estimate of wife-beating occurrences as between one in one hundred to one in two hundred marriages. Gregory[21] also cites Ashley[1] who believes there are between 20,000 and 50,000 cases of wife beating each year in England. While Van Stolk[69] reported that Canada was not recording wife beating as late as 1971, Schlessinger[54] estimates that there are 50,000 battered wives in metropolitan Toronto. Schlessinger[54] also notes that between 10 percent and 30 percent of all police cases in Canada are related to family disputes.

Perhaps the only comparative data on violence toward wives are homicide statistics for various countries. Lystad[69] notes that 70 percent of the murders in Portugal occur in the home, and the single largest category of homicide in Denmark is among family members.

Kumagai and Straus[31] have conducted the only cross–cultural study of spousal violence and report that there is less husband-to-wife violence in Japan and India than in the United States. The rates of husband-to-wife violence are found to be about equal in the three countries studied by Kumagai and Straus.[31]

Even with no reliable baseline data on spousal violence around the world, many investigators have concluded that women are the most likely victims of spousal violence in many, if not all countries.[10,33]

Factors Associated with Family Violence

Child Abuse. As do child-abuse researchers in the United States, researchers in other countries emphasize psychological factors. Low I.Q., psychopathy, abnormal EEG's, emotional disturbances, psychiatric factors, and abnormal personalities have been identified as traits of abusing parents in England and Greece.[35,38,52,56,57]

Researchers in England and Australia have found evidence that abuse is more common in lower socioeconomic groups.[44,56,57] Bhattacharyya[4] states that the causes of abuse in India do not differ from causes in developed countries.

Yet there are some interesting differences between research findings from the developed world and findings in developing nations. Mahmood[37] reports that adolescents are more likely to be abused in India and Arabia, in contrast to other countries where younger children have an increased vulnerability to abuse.[58] More important, as we have noted a number of times, researchers studying abuse in developing nations place considerable emphasis on social change, social disorganization, and cultural attitudes toward children in framing their theories and explanations of child abuse. Social change and the resulting changes in family, tribal, and social organization are seen as important factors causing increases in the occurrence of child abuse in Africa, Greece, and other developing areas.[11] Taylor and Newberger,[65] examining child abuse and neglect cross-culturally, and Fraser and Kilbride,[11] studying abuse among the Samia, note that abuse is less likely to take place in societies that highly value children. Regrettably, these authors provide very little in the way of hard, empirical, comparative data to support their conclusions.

Spouse Abuse. Studies of spouse abuse in other countries also developed parallel to research on spouse abuse in the United States. As in the United States, few, if any, studies done in other countries of violence toward women examine personality, emotional, or other psychological correlates with wife beating. Researchers in Canada, however, have considered alcohol abuse a prime factor accompanying violence toward Canadian wives.[7,18,69]

Similarities between findings in the United States and other countries include: abuse as more common in lower class households,[18] the special vulnerability of pregnant women to abuse,[69] and the intergenerational transmission of violence.[21] A major deviation from U.S. findings was Kumagai's report that social class was *not* related to spousal violence in Japan. [30] Kumagai found that a husband's interactional resources were more important than class or power in explaining violence towards wives.

As noted earlier, European and African studies of the abuse of women place a great deal of emphasis on cultural factors. Mushanga[41] notes that cultures which have strong negative sanctions for wife abuse have low rates of homicide. Loizos,[33] commenting on spouse abuse in Greece, Portugal, Sicily, and Cyprus, explains that violence is considered a legitimate means of punishing women who violate cultural norms concerning family rules and behavior. Dobash and Dobash,[10] citing extensively from historical and cross-cultural documents, make a strong case that women are the prime targets of family violence because of patriarchal cultural values.

In summary, one can draw only tentative conclusions about the patterns of factors related to family violence around the world. In many cases, the definitions of violence used by different investigators are not comparable, nor are their research designs and methods of using their definitions. Often, statements about which factors are, or are not, associated with abuse and violence are based on sketchy data, if they are based on any data at all. Just as methodological and definitional problems limit our knowledge about the extent of family violence around the world, so do they limit our understanding of the similarities and differences among the factors related to violence in various cultures.

References

1. Ashley, J. *Report of House of Commons Debate.* Hansard, July 17, 1973, pp. 218–227.

2. Bamford, F. "Medical diagnosis in non-accidental injury of children," in *Violence in the Family,* pp. 50–60. Edited by M. Borland. New Jersey: Humanities Press, 1976.

3. Beaulieu, L. "Violence and the family: A Canadian view," in *Family Violence: An International and Interdisciplinary Study,* pp. 58–68. Edited by J. Eekelarr and S. Katz. Toronto: Butterworths, 1978.

4. Bhattacharyya, A.K. "Child abuse in India and nutritionally battered child." *Child Abuse and Neglect* 3(2, 1979):607–614.

5. Brandon, S. "Physical violence in the family: An overview," in *Violence in the Family,* pp. 1–25. Edited by M. Borland. New Jersey: Humanities Press, 1976.

6. Buchanan, A. and Oliver, J. "Abuse and neglect as a cause of mental retardation: A study of 140 children admitted to subnormality hospitals in Wiltshire." *Child Abuse and Neglect* 3(2, 1979):467–475.

7. Byles, J. "Family violence in Hamilton." *Canada's Mental Health* 28 (2, 1980): 4–6.

8. Chester, R. and Streather, J. "Cruelty in English divorce: Some empirical findings." *Journal of Marriage and the Family* 34 (November, 1972): 706–712.

9. Christoffel, K., Liu, K., and Stamler, J. "Epidemiology of fatal child abuse: International mortality data." Journal of Chronic Diseases 34(2–3, 1981):57–64.

10. Dobash, R. and Dobash, R. *Violence Against Wives.* New York: Fress Press, 1979.

11. Fraser, G. and Kilbride, P. "Child abuse and neglect—Rare, but perhaps increasing, phenomena among the Samia of Kenya." *Child Abuse and Neglect* 4(4, 1980):227–232.

12. Freeman, M. "The phenomenon of wife battering and the legal and social response in England," in *Family Violence: An International and Interdisciplinary Study,* pp. 73–109. Edited by J. Eekelarr and S. Katz. Toronto: Butterworths, 1978.

13. Gammon, M.B. "The battered baby syndrome: A reconceptualization of family conflict," in *Violence in Canada,* pp. 92–111. Edited by M.B. Gammon. Toronto: Methuen, 1978.

14. Gayford, J. "Wife battering: A preliminary survey of 100 cases." *British Medical Journal* 1(January, 1975):194–197.

15. Gelles, R. "Child abuse as psychopathology: A sociological critique and reformulation." *American Journal of Orthopsychiatry* 43 (July, 1973): 611–621.

16. Gelles, R.J. "The social construction of child abuse." *American Journal of Orthopsychiatry* 45 (April, 1975):363–371.

17. Gelles, R. "Violence in the family: A review of research in the seventies." *Journal of Marriage and the Family* 43 (November, 1980):873–885.

18. Gerson, L. "Alcohol-related acts of violence: who was drinking and where the acts occurred." *Journal of Studies on Alcohol* 39 (July, 1978):1294–1296.

19. Gil, D. *Violence Against Children: Physical Child Abuse in the United States.* Cambridge: Harvard University Press, 1970.

20. Giovannoni, J. and Becerra, R. *Defining Child Abuse.* New York: Free Press, 1979.

21. Gregory, M. "Battered wives," in *Violence in the Family,* pp. 107–128. Edited by M. Borland. New Jersey: Humanities Press, 1976.

22. Gurry, D. "Child abuse: Thoughts on doctors, nurses and prevention," *Child Abuse and Neglect* 1(2–4, 1977):435–443.

23. Guthkelch, A. "Infantile subdural haematoma and its relationship to whiplash injuries." *British Medical Journal* 2 (May, 1971):430–431.

24. Haffner, S. "Wife abuse in Germany." *Victimology* 2(3–4, 1977–78): 472–476.

25. Hyman, C. "Preliminary study of mother/infant interaction." *Child Abuse and Neglect* 1(2–4, 1977):315–320.

26. Jinadu, M. "The role of neglect in the aeteology of protein-energy malnutrition in urban communities of Nigeria." *Child Abuse and Neglect* 4 (4, 1980):233–245.

27. Kamerman, S. "Eight countries: Cross national perspectives on child abuse and neglect." *Children Today* 4 (May–June, 1975):34–37.

28. Kempe, C.H. "Recent developments in the field of child abuse." *Child Abuse and Neglect* 2(4, 1978):261–267.

29. Kempe, C.H. et al. "The battered-child syndrome." *Journal of the American Medical Association* 181 (July, 1962):17–24.

30. Kumagai, F. "Field theory and conjugal violence in Japan," Unpublished manuscript.

31. Kumagai, F. and Straus, M.A. "Conflict resolution tactics in Japan, India, and the U.S.A.," unpublished manuscript.

32. Loening, W. "Child abuse among the Zulus: A people in transition." *Child Abuse and Neglect* 5(1, 1981):3–7.

33. Loizos, P. "Violence and the family: Some Mediterranean examples," in *Violence and the Family,* pp. 183–196. Edited by J. Martin. Chichester: Wiley, 1978.

34. Lynch, M. "The follow-up of abused children: A researcher's nightmare," in *Family Violence: An International and Interdisciplinary Study,* pp. 269–280. Edited by J. Eekelarr and S. Katz. Toronto: Butterworths, 1978.

35. Lynch, M. and Roberts, J. "Predicting child abuse: Signs of bonding failure in the maternity hospital." *British Medical Journal* 1 (March, 1977): 624–626.

36. Lystad, M.H. "Violence at home: A review of the literature." *American Journal of Orthopsychiatry* 45 (April, 1975):328–345.

37. Mahmood, T. "Child abuse in Arabia, India, and the West: Comparative legal aspects," in *Family Violence: An International and Interdisciplinary Study,* pp. 281–289. Edited by J. Eekelarr and S. Katz. Toronto: butterworth, 1978.

38. Maroulis, H. "Child abuse: The Greek scene." *Child Abuse and Neglect* 3(1, 1979):185–190.

39. Marsden, D. and Owens, D. "The Jeckyll and Hyde marriages." *New Society* 32 (May, 1975):333–335.

40. Miniford, A. "Child abuse presenting as apparent 'near-miss' sudden infant death syndrome." *British Medical Journal* 282 (February, 1981):521.

41. Mushanga, T. "Wife victimization in East and Central Africa." *Victimology* 2(3–4, 1977–78):479–485.

42. Nelson, B. "Setting the public agenda: The case of child abuse," in *The Policy Cycle,* pp. 17–41. Edited by J. May and A. Wildavsky. Beverly Hills: Sage, 1978.

43. Newberger, E. et al. "Pediatric social illness: Toward an etiologic classification." *Pediatrics* 60 (August, 1977):178–185.

44. Nixon, J. and Pearn, J. "Non-accidental immersion in the bath: Another extension to the syndrome of child abuse and neglect." *Child Abuse and Neglect* 1(2–4, 1977):445–448.

45. Oates, R., Davis, A. and Ryan, M. "Predictive factors for child abuse." *Australian Paediatric Journal* 16 (December, 1980):239–243.

46. Oliver, J. "Microcephaly following baby battering and shaking." *British Medical Journal* 2 (May, 1975):262–264.

47. Olmesdahl, M. "Parental power and child abuse: An historical and cross-cultural study," in *Family Violence: An International and Interdisciplinary Study,* pp. 253–268. Edited by J. Eekelarr and S. Katz. Toronto: Butterworths, 1978.

48. Oyemade, A. "Child care practices in Nigeria—An urgent plea for social workers." *Child Abuse and Neglect* 4(2, 1980):101–103.

49. Paterson, C. "Ostergenesis imperfecta in the differential diagnosis of child abuse." *Child Abuse and Neglect* 1(2–4, 1977):449–452.

50. Pizzy, E. *Scream Quietly or the Neighbors Will Hear.* Great Britain: Penguin, 1974.

51. Roberts, J. and Hawton, K. "Child abuse and attempted suicide." *British Journal of Psychiatry* 137 (October, 1980):319–323.

52. Rogers, D. et al. "Non-accidental poisoning: An extended syndrome of child abuse." *British Medical Journal* 1 (April, 1976):793–796.

53. Rosendorf, S., ed. "Child maltreatment in the Third World discussed at International Congress on Child Abuse and Neglect." *Children, Youth and Family News* (July, 1981):4.

54. Schlessinger, B. "Abused wives: Canada's silent screamers." *Canada's Mental Health* 28(2, 1980):17–20.

55. Schultz, L. "The wife assaulter." *Journal of Social Therapy* 6(2, 1960):103–111.

56. Smith, S., Honigsberger, L., and Smith, C. "E.E.G. and personality factors in baby batterers." *British Medical Journal* 2 (July, 1973):20–22.

57. Smith, S., Hanson, R., and Nobel, S. "Parents of battered babies: A controlled study." *British Medical Journal* 4 (November, 1973):388–391.

58. Smith, S. and Hanson, R. "134 battered children: A medical and psychological study." *British Medical Journal* 3 (September, 1974):666–670.

59. Snell, J., Rosenwald, R. and Robey, A. "The wife beater's wife: A study of family interaction." *Archives of General Psychiatry* 11 (August, 1964):107–113.

60. Speight, A., Bridson, J., and Cooper, C. "Follow-up survey of cases of child abuse seen at Newcastle General Hospital 1974–75." *Child Abuse and Neglect* 3(2, 1979):555–563.

61. Straus, M., Gelles, R. and Steinmetz, S. *Behind Closed Doors: Violence in the American Family.* Garden City, N.Y.: Anchor Press;Doubleday, 1980.

62. Straus, P. and Girodet, D. "Three French follow-up studies on abused children." *Child Abuse and Neglect* 1(1, 1977):99–103.

63. Tangen, O. "Medical ethics and the maltreatment of children—100

years after." *Child Abuse and Neglect* 1(2–4, 1977):257–268.

64. Tauber, E., Meda, C., and Vitro, V. "Child ill-treatment as considered by the Italian criminal and civil codes." *Child Abuse and Neglect* 1(1, 1977): 149–152.

65. Taylor, L. and Newberger, E. "Child abuse in the International year of the child." *New England Journal of Medicine* 301 (November, 1979): 1205–1212.

66. Turbett, J. and O'Toole, R. "Physician's recognition of child abuse," paper presented at the annual meetings of the American Sociological Association, New York, 1980.

67. Van Rees, R. "Five years of child abuse as a symptom of family problems," in *Family Violence: An International and Interdisciplinary Study,* pp. 329–337. Edited by J. Eekelarr and S. Katz. Toronto: Butterworths, 1978.

68. Van Staden, J. "The mental development of abused children in South Africa." *Child Abuse and Neglect* 3(3–4, 1979):997–1000.

69. Van Stolk, M. "Beaten women, battered children." *Children Today* 5 (March–April, 1976):8–12.

70. Van Stolk, M. *The Battered Child in Canada.* Toronto: The Canadian Publishers, 1978.

71. Vesterdal, J. "Handling child abuse in Denmark." *Child Abuse and Neglect* 2(1, 1977):193–198.

72. Vesterdal, J. "Psychological mechanisms in child-abusing parents," in *Family Violence: An International and Interdisciplinary Study,* pp. 290–294. Edited by J. Eekelarr and S. Katz. Toronto: Butterworths, 1978.

73. Vinocur, J. "Sweden's anti-spanking law is something of a hit." *The New York Times,* 19 October 1980, sec. 1, p. 22.

Part I
Cross-Cultural Examinations
of Family Violence

Introduction to Part I

This section contains a small but significant group of papers that examine child abuse, wife abuse, and family violence from a cross-cultural perspective. The current state of the art of research on family violence is such that these few papers constitute much of the available literature examining family violence cross culturally.[1]

Straus's chapter, "Societal Morphogenesis and Intrafamily Violence in Cross–Cultural Perspective," continues his earlier presentations which argue that intrafamily violence is neither rare nor confined to mentally ill persons. When Straus authored this paper, the notion that violence was widespread among families in the United States was relatively new and controversial. Having convincingly demonstrated the prevalence of violence in American families, Straus makes the challenging assertion that family violence is "near universal." If this is true, Straus contends, a social phenomenon with this kind of frequency must somehow be related to the most fundamental aspects of human association. This is a direct challenge to theories of family violence that attempt to assess the causes of violence and abuse at the level of individuals.

Taylor and Newberger's review of child abuse around the globe does not attempt to support Straus's claim that family violence is near universal. But clearly, the historical and cross–cultural record of child rearing is marked by cruel and widespread victimization of children. Taylor and Newberger find some variation in the types, manifestations, and extent of child victimization around the world. The cross–cultural literature reviewed by Taylor and Newberger also reveals variations in actions taken to prevent and treat child maltreatment in developed and undeveloped nations.

Sheila Kamerman reports on the results of an eight–country cross-cultural survey carried out in 1972. The eight countries were all developed nations, and the study was designed to assess definitions, legislation, policy, and programs for dealing with child abuse. The article is rich in cross–cultural comparisons, and the great tragedy is that this study has not been repeated since 1972.

The final article in this section is a unique and valuable examination of the relationship between wife beating and the punishment of women. Levinson, using data from the Human Relations Area Files, assesses whether wife beating is linked to the punishment of children. One of his conclusions is that women, not children, are the most frequent victims of family violence. This conclusion is consistent with the discussions presented in Part III of this book, which examine spouse abuse.

Note

1. The most complete cross-cultural and historical assessment of patterns of violence towards women can be found in Dobash and Dobash, *Violence Against Wives*. New York: Free Press, 1979.

2

Societal Morphogenesis and Intrafamily Violence in Cross-Cultural Perspective[a]

Murray A. Straus

"How do I know that he loves me if he doesn't beat me?"[37]

(Statement by a Mangaia wife)

"What makes you think he doesn't love you any more?" asks a woman on a BBC program in the spring of 1974. The reply: "He hasn't bashed me in a fortnight."

There is an obvious similarity between what these two inhabitants of such vastly dissimilar islands are saying: namely, that the marital relationship is tinged by physical aggression, to say nothing of other forms of aggression.[b]

Reprinted with permission from The New York Academy of Sciences. M.A. Straus, "Societal morphogenesis and intrafamily violence in cross-cultural perspective," in *Issues in Cross-Cultural Research*, pp. 717–730. Edited by Leonore Loeb Adler, 1977.

[a]This paper is part of a research program on intrafamily violence supported by grants from the National Institute of Mental Health; specifically Grant No. MH 15521 for research training in family and deviance and Grant No. MH 27557 for a study of physical violence in American families. A list of the program publications is available on request.

[b]The concepts of aggression, violence, and war are the subject of considerable controversy and definitional confusion. It is beyond the scope of this paper to resolve even part of this conceptual problem (but see Gelles and Straus[23]). However, I can at least make clear the sense in which I am using these terms:

Aggression: An act carried out with the intent of, or which is perceived as being with the intent of, injuring another person. The injury may be of many kinds, including psychological, material deprivation, or physical injury. It can range from minor noxious acts, such as a disparaging look, to murder.

There are many other dimensions that must be considered and specified in addition to the dimensions of "motivation," "attribution," "type of injury," and "seriousness of injury" just mentioned. Much of the confusion and seemingly contradictory findings in aggression research probably occurs because these dimensions are not specified. Among these other dimensions are the degree of normative legitimacy, and the extent to which the aggression is "instrumental" to some other purpose, versus "expressive" i.e., carried out as an end in itself.

Violence: An act carried out with the intent of, or which is perceived as being with the intent of, *physically* injuring another person. A more specific and less value-laden term is "physical aggression."

War: Formally organized armed combat between groups of people who constitute territorial teams or political communities.[26,45]

27

The fact that the marital relationship is also often characterized by warmth, affection, or solidarity is not inconsistent with the simultaneous existence of aggression because aggressive acts can be counternormative, or because norms permitting or encouraging aggression between spouses can and do exist simultaneously with norms stressing warmth and solidarity.[64]

I began this paper with these two quotations because they dramatically illustrate the high frequency—or perhaps even the near universality—with which aggression and violence of all types occur within the family. Obviously, I need hardly comment to a group such as this on the danger of referring to any phenomenon as a "cross-cultural universal." Not even those social forms to which the term "family" is usually applied are universal, except in the most limited and technical sense suggested by Weigert and Thomas.[69] However, the family in the sense used by Murdock[38] is an example of a social form that is so widespread that it constitutes what might be called a "near universal." A "near universal" obviously does not have the same theoretical importance as a true universal would have—if such existed. But a near universal is none the less extremely important because (by definition) it affects such a large proportion of humanity, and also for theoretical reasons. The theoretical value of attention to near universals stems from the assumption that any social form which occurs that frequently must somehow be related to the most fundamental aspects of human association. Hence the importance of the first objective of this paper: to explore the question of whether intrafamily violence (i.e., physical aggression between family members) is so frequent that it can be considered a near universal. I will also summarize some of the cross-cultural research on the factors that may make intrafamily aggression typical of most societies, and then conclude with a consideration of the wider theoretical import of violence in the family, and specifically, the view that the level of intrafamily violence is related to the ecological conditions in which a society is operating and the society's "technico-economic" adaptation to these ecological realities and to changes in the subsistence basis of the society. I will also suggest that these relationships can be understood best from the perspective of general systems theory because this perspective focuses on morphological changes in society as a model of system maintenance.

The Prevalence of Conjugal Violence

In previous books and papers, my colleagues and I have presented evidence that in the United States—and probably also in most other Euroamerican societies—the family is the preeminent social setting for all types of aggression and violence, ranging from the cutting remark to slaps, kicks, torture, and murder.[22,58,62,63] The frequency of aggressive acts between children (who will often be siblings) is remarkably constant across the societies of the

Six Cultures Study,[32] and probably also including societies such as the !Ko-Bushmen, who are renowned for their nonaggressive and peaceful social patterns.[19] In the United States, Straus found that 62 percent of his sample engaged in a nonplayful physical fight with a sibling during their senior year in high school. Parent-child physical violence is truly ubiquitous in the form of physical punishment, not only in the United States and Britain,[58-60] but also in many other societies, again including the !Ko.[19]

Probably the most dramatic cross-cultural evidence on intrafamily violence is found for murder. Because murder is such an extreme and difficult-to-conceal form of violence, it is the subject of official recording in many societies and is more readily researched in all societies than "ordinary" wife (or husband) beating. Thus, Bohannan[9] and his collaborator were able to collect what seems to be reasonably good statistical evidence in four different African societies. As a result, there is evidence covering a number of societies. This evidence clearly indicates that more murders take place between members of the same family than occur with any other murderer-victim relationship. This assertion holds for all 18 societies for which data are summarized in the recent book by Curtis on criminal violence.[16] To this we can add the findings for the Mexican village studied by June Nash.[40] My tabulation of the data given in her table 2-1 reveals that a family member or lover was the probable killer in 52 percent of the instances in which a suspect was identified.

In considering these statistics on the high proportion of homicides that occur within families, there are numerous complications. For example, although the largest *proportion* of homicides are between kin, and especially husbands and wives, in absolute terms killing one's husband or wife is rare even in those societies that have a high homicide rate. In fact, the figures are somewhat deceptive because there is some tendency for the proportion of all homicides that are intrafamily to be greatest in the societies with a *low* overall homicide rate. For example, the Danish homicide rate is only 0.2 per 100,000 compared to the United States' rate of about 7 or 8 per 100,000. Thus, the very high proportion of within-family homicides in Denmark (57 percent as compared with the United States' figure of about 25 percent) must be seen as a large slice of a very small pie. But perhaps a more telling interpretation of these relationships is the possibility of their having the following meaning: Even in societies such as Denmark, in which homicide has practically been eliminated, the last remaining locus of this form of aggression is within the family.

Less drastic forms of aggression between family members are of course more prevalent in the absolute sense. This can be seen both within American society, where my colleagues and I have been gathering such data, and in a few cross-cultural studies. In the United States, the evidence we have gathered—although tentative—suggests that perhaps 60 to 70 percent of all couples have used physical violence at least once in their marriage, and that for about one out of four couples, there has been a recurring pattern of physical violence between the couple.[22,58,62,63] These rates are somewhat lower for middle-class couples, but not enough lower to support the widely held view that husband-wife violence is primarily found in the lowest socioeconomic strata.

Turning to other societies, my general impression is that high rates of conjugal violence characterize many other societies, including urban-industrial, agrarian, nonliterate societies; and also including societies that are otherwise low in violence, such as England. But on theoretical grounds which I will come to shortly, we can expect the highest rates of husband-wife violence to be in those societies which have high rates of violence in other institutional spheres. Thus, it is doubtful that many other societies could match the frequency and intensity of assaults by husbands on their wives than is found among "the fierce people" as the Yanomamo call themselves.[8,14] Finally, we can gain some idea of the prevalence of conjugal violence from Schlegel's ratings of 45 societies.[54] Her analysis reveals that 75 percent of these societies permitted husbands to aggress against their wives. On the other hand, I do not know how representative Schlegel's 45 societies are, and only a relatively limited number of more detailed ethnographies are cited at various places in this paper. So, although what evidence there is points to high rates of conjugal violence in a great many societies, the question of the "prevalence," much less of the "near-universality" of intrafamily violence, is far from definitively established.

The Causes of Conjugal Violence

A full causal explanation of the ubiquity of conjugal violence is a vast undertaking. Richard Gelles and I have made a start in that direction in a long chapter of a forthcoming book.[23] For example, among the factors we examined in that paper are (1) *"Time at risk,"* i.e., the fact that in many societies family members spend considerable amounts of time with each other. Other things being equal, they therefore are more likely to engage in disputes and conflicts with each other than with those whom they spend less time. But of course, other things are not equal, and particularly: (2) Family members are likely to share a wider *range of activities and interests* with each than with others with whom they may also spend much time. This means that there are more "events" over which a dispute or a failure to meet expectations can occur. (3) Not only is there a greater probability of hurting family members than others because of the greater time exposure and the greater number of spheres of overlapping activity and interests, but in addition, the degree of injury experienced when the problem arises with a family member is greater than when it arises with someone else because of the *intensity of involvement and attachment* that is typical of family relationships. (4) *Sexual inequality* and the typical pattern of ascribed superior position for the husband has a high conflict potential built in because it is inevitable that not all husbands will be able to perform the culturally expected leadership role and/or not all wives will be willing to accept the subordinate role.[1] The *privacy* of the family in many societies insulates it both from assistance in coping with intrafamily disputes and from social control by neighbors and other kin. This factor is, of course, most present in the conjugal family of urban-industrial societies and least present among societies such as the Bushmen, where virtually all of family life is carried within the small circle of the Bushmen camp and is open to immediate intercession by others. (6) Cultural norms legitimizing the use of violence between members of the same family in situations that would make violence a serious normative violation if it occurred outside the family. In Euroamerican societies, to this day, there is a strong, though largely unverbalized, norm that makes the marriage licence also a hitting licence.[64]

Each of the above, together with other factors, merits detailed consideration. However, within the confines of this paper there is only room to consider those causal factors that have been empirically studied in at least two societies. Although this is not adequate theoretical basis for selection, it has the merits of being appropriate for the focus of this conference and of reducing the range of materials to be considered to what can be fitted within the pages of a single paper.

Aggression as a Cultural and Structural Pattern

I have already alluded to what may be the most general causal factor. This is the fact that, as Russell[52] notes on the basis of a factor analysis of 78 variables for the societies in Textor's Cross Cultural Summary,[65] "... all forms of aggression tend to be strongly related to each other." This finding and its theoretical explication stand in sharp contrast to drive theories of aggression. Drive theories assume that aggression expressed in one sphere of activity will —roughly to that extent—not be expressed in other spheres of social interaction. Steinmetz and I[59] have elsewhere called this the "catharsis myth" because of the large number of studies that not only fail to support the idea of catharsis, but that almost always show exactly the opposite: that the more aggression in one sphere, the more in others.

Excellent and devastating reviews of the research on aggression catharsis at the individual level have been published by Bandura,[5] Berkowitz,[7] and Hokanson,[28] and a study by Straus[62] of within-family "ventilation" of aggression shows clearly that verbal, symbolic, and physical aggression, rather than being substitutes for each other, are highly correlated. Consequently, in this paper I will mention only cross–cultural studies that bear on aggression as a pervasive cultural pattern. An interesting starting place is Sipes'[56] study of the relationship between aggressive sports and warfare. He shows that both cross–culturally and in a time-series analysis for the United States, the higher the level of armed combat, the more common are aggressive sports. Vayda's review of anthropological explanations of primitive warfare and aggression is also critical of the catharsis theory.[68] A study by Archer and Gartner[2] of 110 nations find that, contrary to the catharsis theory, homicide rates increase with the occurrence of war. In respect to the mass media, the nations or periods with the most actual violence are those with the most violent popular literature.[15,29,54] Finally, in respect to husband-wife violence itself, Steinmetz [57] studied the families of university students in an American and a Canadian city using identical instruments. She wanted to compare Canadian and American families because these two societies are alike in so many ways, yet Canadian rates for homicide, assault and rape and only a fraction of the rates in the United States. The Canadian families turned out to have a considerably lower frequency of husband-wife physical aggression. I conclude from these and other studies that each modality of aggression in a society, rather than serving as a means of "draining off hostility," serves as a means to learn aggressive roles and as a kind of cultural and structural "theme,"[44] template, or paradigm for interaction in other spheres of activity.[c]

Aggression as a Family Pattern

The same theoretical principle also applies *within* the family. That is, violence in one family role is associated with violence in other family roles. Thus, stud-

---

[c]Concepts such as "theme" and "pattern" have come into disrepute because they are associated with a kind of mystical "cultural determinism" which diverts attention from the issue of *why* a particular cultural pattern came into being and why it continues to exist. However, this needed reaction to such concepts has "thrown the baby out with the bath water." One need not deny the existence of culture as system manifesting themes and interrelated patterns in order to deal with the questions of why such a cultural system exists and how it operates. In fact, I take the view that unless one can identify cultural themes and patterns, the likelihood of understanding the more fundamental causes of the most basic aspects of a society is greatly diminished. An additional reason for not discarding the concept of a cultural pattern is that, in my belief, once in existence, such a pattern has a causal efficacy of its own, exerting influence on other aspects of the culture, personality, and social organization of a society. That assertion has also come into disrepute because it is so often associated with a static "functionalist" view of human society. But that is a particular historical accident of a certain period in the history of social science. My view of the relationships between the biological, cultural, personality and social organizational systems is that each is constantly changing and therefore creating discrepancies or discordancies that are resolved by still further changes. Thus, the assumption of functional integration within and between these spheres directs attention to processes of social change rather than social stasis.

ies of child-abusing parents in three countries found that such parents had themselves experienced severe physical punishment as children.[47] At the macro level of analysis, although child-abuse statistics can be best considered only as educated guesses, there seems to be some correlation with the frequency with which physical punishment occurs in a society. Goode,[24] for example, suggests that child abuse is rare in Japan because physical punishment is rarely used. Finally, the study by Steinmetz of United States' and Canadian families found that couples who use physical force on each other use physical punishment more often than other couples. Moreover, their children, in turn, use physical aggression against siblings more often than do the children of parents who do not hit each other.

Protest Masculinity

There is an impressive group of studies—both cross-cultural and studies within a number of societies—which suggest that what might be called "psychological father absence" or low saliency of the father during infancy or childhood leads to a pattern of male behavior that has variously been called protest masculinity, hyperaggressive masculinity, compulsive masculinity, etc. It is probably most widely known to social scientists in the United States as the complex of traits characterizing the *machismo* pattern of many Latin American males. The low saliency of the father is most obvious in mother-child households, but it is sometimes possible for the father to be a salient figure in the lives of children even if he is not physically present, as in the *kibbutzim.* Conversely, the father can be physically but not psychologically present, as often happens in the extremely sex-role-differentiated pattern of the urban lower class.

Low father saliency—however it is manifested—has been found to be associated with such traits as a preference for segregated sex roles, subordination of women, aggressive sexuality, and the glorification of physical aggression.[4,10,21,27,36,66,70] Within the family, this manifests itself in a high frequency of wife-beating, and cross-culturally is also associated with probably the most violent marital arrangement of all—true bride-theft as opposed to mock bride-theft.[3] Ayres summarizes the theory accounting for these relationships as follows:

> The widely accepted explanation for these relationships is that such behaviors represent exaggerated attempts to demonstrate masculinity by individuals who have a high level of sex identity conflict and anxiety. This conflict arises when individuals who have formed an initial feminine identification during infancy come into contact with society's demand that adult males show

assertive behavior and assume dominant status. The resulting initiation ceremonies, crime and deliquency, are interpreted as resolving the conflict and
enhancing the individual's sense of masculinity.[d]

Intrafamily Violence

Male Dominance

Since I have elsewhere devoted most of two entire papers to the issue of the
linkage between sexual inequality and wife-beating in just one society,[1,64]
it is clear that only the briefest summary of the complex links between male
dominance and intrafamily violence can be presented here. Probably the best
place to begin is with Schlegel's finding that 88 percent of the male-dominant
societies in her sample permitted aggression by husbands against wives, as
compared to only 33 percent of the non-male-dominant societies.[54]

A number of factors underlie this relationship, starting with the simple
fact that men in all societies have superior physical strength as an ultimate
resource to enforce a superior position, and they make frequent use of this
resource.[1] However, as Harris[25,26] notes, the physical-strength advantage
is relatively slight and by itself does not seem to be an adequate explanation
since superior strength is unnecessary to make effective use of knives and male
infanticide. Very likely, as Harris suggests, the institution of warfare is an important underlying factor and this in turn is related to such things as the antag-
onism between the sexes engendered by sex role segregation[70] and the
inability of women to escape from a violent husband in many societies, including most Euroamerican societies. Such societies throw the full burden of
child-rearing on women, deny them equal job opportunities even when they
can make alternative child-care arrangements, inculcate a negative self image
in roles other than that of wife and mother, and reinforce the dependency of
women on their husbands by emphasizing the idea that divorce is bad for children. Finally, in most societies, there is a male-oriented legal and judicial system, which makes it extremely difficult for women to secure legal protection
from assault by their husbands except under the most extreme circumstances.

---

[d]Professor Ayres has also pointed out to me that the causal sequence in respect to societal change (as compared to the causal sequence for individuals at one point in history)
can equally plausibly go from aggressive masculinity to sex-role segregation and low
father-saliency. Such an interpretation, in fact, is consistent with Harris' theory of
male dominance and female infanticide as adaptations to the institutions of warfare.[25,26]

Intrafamily Aggression and Group Survival

Many hunting and gathering societies such as the Eskimo and the !Ko-Bush-
men are noted for their peacefulness and lack of physical aggression. A distinctive trait of such societies is their openness and sharing. Yet these same
societies also provide an instructive example of intrafamily aggression. First,
it is clear from both cross-cultural studies of the correlates of war and aggressiveness and from detailed ethnographies, that a primary basis of their peacefulness is to be found in the cross-cutting group affiliations inherent in the
kinship system and in the system of food-sharing. Or, as Eibl-Eibesfeldt puts
it in relation to the !Ko, "What is striking when observing the Bushmen is not
their lack of aggression, but their efficient way of coping with it."[19] The
second instructive feature of this type of society is to be found in their response
to famine. When, as in the case of the Eskimo, the normal subsistence base of
the society is precarious, the culturally evolved response calls for intrafamily
aggression in the form of abandonment of the old and infanticide.[c] In addition,
when the subsistence base is further reduced, new forms of competitiveness
and aggression may appear, as illustrated by Riches'[50] work on the effects
of "environmental stress" among the Netsilik Eskimo, and Opler's on Apache
witchcraft. Probably the most dramatic example is the Ik, as described by
Turnbull.[67] The food-sharing reciprocity that lies at the heart of the non-
aggressiveness of such foraging societies became impossible and many social
bonds disintegrated with a resultant almost unspeakable cruelty and callous-
ness; for example, watching with amusement as a crawling child puts his hand
in a fire, leaving children as young as three years old to fend for themselves,
and children and young men pushing over a group of tottering old men as

---

[c]Some readers may question categorizing abandonment and infanticide as "aggression"
because they are culturally legitimate acts, necessary for group survival. My position
is that the normative approval versus disapproval of an injurious act is an important
but separate dimension that must be separately analyzed. There are numerous other
instances of normatively legitimate aggression, ranging from physical punishment by
parents to the bombing of Hanoi, the former being legitimized because it is presumably necessary for the welfare of the child, and for the society as a whole, for parents to
be able to control and train children; and the latter because it was presumably necessary
for national survival in the face of a world communist threat. Obviously, I have picked
these examples because they also indicate that the question of normative legitimacy is
itself extremely complex, especially when one faces up to the fact that there is seldom
unanimity concerning these norms.[23] In addition, the fact that the overwhelming
majority of Americans approve of physical punishment, and favored the bombing of
North Vietnam, does not place them outside the scope of "aggression" as defined earlier
in this paper. Finally, I should point out that Harris[26] also considers infanticide as
aggression when he defines it as ". . . homicide and acts of malign and benign aggression and neglect that consciously or unconsciously [affect] . . . survival . . ." of an infant.

though they were bowling pins, and shrieking with laughter as the old men fell and struggled to stand up.

I disagree with Turnbull's suggestion that the destruction of the Ik economy and the resulting cruelty and inhumanity reveal the basic feature of human nature. Their aggressiveness under these circumstances is no more—and no less—indicative of human nature than was their peacefulness and sharing when food was plentiful. Rather, what the Ik and the Eskimo tell us is that the level of aggression within families is governed by the complex interrelation of the constraints and resources of the particular ecological niche occupied by a society, the social organization of that society that evolved in relation to their particular ecological niche, the position of the family in that social organization, and the behavioral and personality characteristics that are congruent with these life circumstances.

Summary and Conclusions

If time permitted, a similar analysis to the one just presented could be developed for parent-child and sibling-sibling violence. Indeed, in pointing out the isomorphism between the level of violence in the husband-wife role and the parent-child role, a start has already been made in that direction. Similarly, just as the level of physical aggression in the conjugal relationship tends to be isomorphic with the level of physical aggression in nonfamily spheres of life, the same principle seems to hold for the parental relationship.[6,33,45,46]

A detailed analysis of parent-child and sibling-sibling violence—and also of aggression and sexuality—along the lines of the suggestive paper by Prescott[49] would strengthen the case for the theoretical conclusions I am about to put forth because they would add processes that are specific to violence in these relationships, yet at the same time are illustrative of the more general theory. For example, this would include analysis of the fact that (1) within-society, the larger the number of children in a household, the greater the use of physical punishment;[20,34,41–43] and (2) of the social class differences in the frequency and purposes of physical punishment.[12,17,18,30,31,34,39,48] But even without this additional evidence, the analysis of conjugal violence presented in this paper suggests the following theoretical conclusions:

I began the paper with the assumption that it is important to study near-universals of human social behavior because any social form that occurs that frequently must somehow be related to the most fundamental aspects of human society. One of the fundamental features that this paper illustrates is the fact that human societies are cybernetic and morphogenic systems operating as part of a larger ecological system.[f] The materials presented show five

---

[f]Readers of this paper who are anthropologists might find the concept "evolution" preferable (or at least more familiar) than the concept of "morphogenesis." I use the latter term because I do not want to confuse processes of cultural and social organiza-

aspects of this: the first three illustrating systemic linkages and the last two morphogenic processes: (1) The link between aggression and violence in the society and the level of violence within the family. I suggest that this is in the form of a positive feedback relationship: as societal violence increases, there is a tendency for intrafamily violence to increase; and as intrafamily violence increases, there is a tendency for societal violence to increase. Harris' interpretation of the changes in Yanomamo society over the past 100 or so years[26] seems to illustrate such processes. (2) The link between violence in one family role with violence in other family roles, which is also a positive feedback relationship. There are a number of reasons for this, including the tendency to respond to violence by violence (if the situation permits), role-modeling, and generalization of behavior patterns learned in one role to other roles ("transfer of training").[g] (3)The identification of the system-maintaining contributions of intrafamily violence, as illustrated in the emergence of "protest masculinity" on the part of young men whose sexual identity is made problematic because of household structure or other circumstances of child-rearing; and also as illustrated by the use or threat of physical force to maintain the structure of male dominance. (4) The change from a nonviolent to a violent structure of interaction as an adaption to changes in the critical exogenous variable of the subsistence basis of the society as illustrated by the Ik and the Yanomamo. (5) Changes in personality as actors adapt to the new behaviors required by the changed structure of interaction, which, in turn, brings about changes in other spheres of interaction. Since this last point has only indirectly been hinted at in the paper, I will close by discussing the morphogenic processes that are mediated through changes in the personality of members of a society.

---

tional change (the focus of this paper) with biological change processes, however analogous the two may seem to be. I have also chosen the concept of morphogenesis because it is consistent with a "general systems theory" (as opposed to a functionalist systems theory) framework, and I want these comments and speculations to be understood within the former framework. There are many subtle but extremely important differences between these two seemingly similar theoretical perspectives.[13,61] However, for the present purposes, the difference that is most crucial concerns the morphostatic focus of functionalist theory versus the emphasis on morphogenesis in general systems theory. In the former, the analyst asks how the system can adapt to internal and external influences and retain its basic *goals,* one of the most frequent adaptive mechanisms being a change in structure.

[g]Although I have emphasized positive feedback processes, it is equally important to identify "dampening" or negative feedback processes, which sooner or later must enter the picture. For an illustration of such negative feedback loops in relation to intrafamily violence in the United States see Straus.[61] Looked at cross-culturally, the issue becomes one of identifying the factors that make the upper limit of permissible violence vary from society to society, one of which has already been mentioned: Whether the victims of intrafamily violence (more typically women than men) have an alternative to tolerating aggression by their spouse. If the structure of the society provides other marriage opportunities, or the possibility of return to the wife's natal family, it seems likely that this will impose an upper limit on the level of violence that will be

For a variety of reasons the rate of internal or external warfare can increase sharply, or a previously peaceful society can become involved in either external war or internal feuds. If this happens, members of the society must learn to behave more aggressively, as a matter of both individual and group survival. This may be what happened in the case of the Yanomamo and the Ik. But the aggressive behavior patterns learned as a means of carrying out war or internal conflict are not easily turned off when it comes to relationships within the family. That is, such a situation brings about personality characteristics that exert a strain toward isomorphism between patterns of social interaction between and within families. Of course, one must not put the whole burden of change-producing linkages on the mechanism of intraindividual carryover of personality. Other social institutions are also important, as is shown by the studies of the correlation between conceptions of supernatural beings as benevolent or malevolent with indices of warfare and aggression and of punitiveness in child training;[33,46] studies that show that sports (and in literate societies, fiction) are also related to warfare;[29,56] and the integration of the religious, ecological, and warfare systems of the Tsembaga Maring.[51]

In conclusion, this paper has dealt with both the external changes faced by society and the internal conflicts and systematic linkages that are equally a part of social life. In the history of a society (sometimes even over as short a period of time as a generation or two), these external changes and internal conflicts can lead to changes in the structure of the society itself as a result of the cybernetic processes by which events are monitored and controlled in accordance with system goals. The tragic case of the Ik provides a dramatic example of morphogenesis in the structure of interpersonal relationships (the system of reciprocity) to serve more fundamental system goals. Turnbull interprets their behavior as reversion to a primitive aggressive individualism. But the reanalysis of his report by McCall[35] and Wilson[71] suggests that, had *individual* survival been the primary goal, the course of events might have been much different: The Ik could have accepted the government's repeated offers to relocate to a "more favorable" location. Instead, the deep attachment of the Ik to their society and to its sacred territory and way of life led them to the almost unimaginable cruelties against each other (particularly the old and the young), and to drastic changes in the pattern of interaction so that the essential nature of their society, as they saw it, could be maintained.

---

tolerated. Another aspect of this is the importance of the domestic group and/or lineage itself. Sahlins, for example, acknowledges that ". . . considering interpersonal relations as such . . . the closer the social bond the greater the hostility[potential]." But paradoxically, he also notes that "The closer the relationship the greater the restraint on belligerence and violence . . ."[53] because the focus of his discussion is societies with a segmentary lineage organization in which the lineage is a property-controlling corporate group on which individual survival depends, and which therefore must be protected from internal disruption.

Acknowledgments

I would like to thank Professor Barbara Ayres of the University of Massachusetts/Boston, and Professors Rand B. Foster and Stephen Reyna of the University of New Hampshire for comments and criticisms that aided in the revision of this paper.

References

1. Allen, C.M. and Straus, M.A. "Resources, power, and husband-wife violence," paper presented at the National Council on Family Relations 1975 Annual Meetings.

2. Archer, D. and Gartner, R. "Violent acts and violent times: A comparative approach to postwar homicide rates." *American Sociological Review* 41 (December, 1976):937–963.

3. Ayres, B. "Bride theft and raiding for wives in cross-cultural perspective." *Anthropological Quarterly* 47 (July, 1974):238–252.

4. Bacon, M.K., Child, I.L., and Barry, H. III. "A cross-cultural study of correlates of crime." *Journal of Abnormal and Social Psychology* 66 (July-Sept., 1963):291–300.

5. Bandura, A. *Aggression: A Social Learning Analysis.* Englewood Cliffs, N.J.: Prentice-Hall, 1973.

6. Bellak, L. and Antell, M. "An intercultural study of aggressive behavior on children's playground." *American Journal of Orthopsychiatry* 44 (July, 1974):503–511.

7. Berkowitz, L. "The case for bottling up rage." *Psychology Today* 7 (July, 1973): 24–31.

8. Biocca, E. *Yanoama: The Story of a Woman Abducted by Brazilian Indians.* London, England: George Allen and Unwin, 1969.

9. Bohannan, P. *African Homicide and Suicide.* New York, N.Y.: Atheneum, 1960.

10. Bohannan, P. "Cross-cultural comparison of aggression and violence," in *Crimes of Violence,* Appendix 25, Vol. 13 of the Staff Reports to the National Commission on the Causes and Prevention of Violence. Edited by Donald Mulvihull and Melvin M. Tumin. Washington, D.C.: U.S. Government Printing Office, 1969.

11. Briggs, J.L. *Never in Anger: Portrait of an Eskimo Family.* Cambridge: Harvard University Press, 1970.

12. Bronfenbrenner, U. "Socialization and social class through time and space," in *Readings in Social Psychology,* pp. 400–425. Edited by E.E. Maccoby, T.M. Newcomb and E.L. Hartley. New York: Holt, 1958.

13. Buckley, W. *Sociology and Modern Systems Theory.* Englewood Cliffs, N.J.: Prentice-Hall, 1967.

14. Chagnon, N.A. *Yanomamo: The Fierce People.* New York: Holt, Rinehart, and Winston, 1968.

15. Comstock, G.A. and Rubinstein, E.A. *Television and Social Behavior. Reports and Papers: A Technical Report to the Surgeon General's Scientific Advisory Committee on Television and Social Behavior, Vol I.* Washington, D.C.: U.S. Government Printing Office, 1972.

16. Curtis, L.A. *Criminal Violence: National Patterns and Behavior.* Lexington, Mass: Lexington Books, 1974.

17. Devereux, E.C. "Socialization in cross-cultural perspective: Comparative study of England, Germany, and the United States," in *Families in East and West,* pp. 72–106. Edited by Reuben Hill and Rene Konig. Paris: Mouton and Co., 1970.

18. Devereux, E.C., Bronfenbrenner, U. and Rodgers, R.R. "Child-rearing in England and the United States: A cross-national comparison." *Journal of Marriage and the Family* 31 (May, 1969): 257–270.

19. Eibl-Eibesfeldt, I. "Aggression in the !Ko-Bushmen," in *Aggression,* pp. 10–17. Edited by S.H. Frazier. Baltimore, Md.: Williams and Wilkens, 1974.

20. Elder, G.H. and Bowerman, C.E. "Family structure and child rearing patterns: The effects of family size and sex composition." *American Sociological Review* 28 (December, 1963):891–905.

21. Ferracuti, F. and Dinitz, S. "Cross-cultural aspects of delinquent and criminal behavior," in *Aggression,* pp. 287–303. Edited by S.H. Frazier. Baltimore, MD.: Williams and Wilkens, 1974.

22. Gelles, R.J. *The Violent Home: A Study of Physical Aggression between Husbands and Wives.* Beverly Hills, Calif.: Sage, 1974.

23. Gelles, R.J. and Straus, M.A. "Determinants of violence in the family: Toward a theoretical integration," in *Contemporary Theories about the Family,* pp. 549–581. Edited by W.R. Burr, R. Hill, I. Nye, and I.L. Reiss. New York: The Free Press, 1977.

24. Goode, W.J. "Force and violence in the family." *Journal of Marriage and the Family* 33 (November, 1971):624–636.

25. Harris, M., ed. "The savage male," in *Cows, Pigs, Wars, and Witches: The Riddles of Culture,* pp. 83–107. New York: Random House, 1974.

26. Harris, M. *Culture, People, Nature: An Introduction to General Anthropology.* 2nd ed. New York: Thomas Y. Crowell, 1975.

27. Hoffman, M.L. "Father absence and conscience development," *Developmental Psychology* 4 (May, 1971):400–406.

28. Hokanson, J.E. "Psychophysiological evaluation of the catharsis hypothesis," in *The Dynamics of Aggression,* pp. 47–86. Edited by E.I. Magargee and J.E. Hokanson. New York: Harper and Row, 1970.

29. Huggins, M.D. and Straus, M.A. "Violence and the social structure as reflected in children's books from 1850 to 1970," paper presented at the 1975 annual meeting of the Eastern Sociological Society.

30. Kearns, B.J. "Childrearing practices among selected culturally deprived minorities." *Journal of Genetic Psychology* 116 (June, 1970):149–155.

31. Kohn, M.L. *Class and Conformity*. Homewood, Ill: Dorsey Press, 1969.

32. Lambert, W.W. "Promise and problems of cross-cultural exploration of children's aggressive strategies," in *Determinants and Origins of Aggressive Behavior,* pp. 444–447. Edited by J. De Wit and W.W. Hartup. The Netherlands: Mouton, 1974.

33. Lambert, W.W., Triandis, L.M. and Wolf, M. "Some correlates of beliefs in the malevolence and benevolence and supernatural beings: A cross-societal study." *Journal of Abnormal and Social and Psychology* 58 (March, 1959):162–169.

34. Light, R. "Abused and neglected children in America: A study of alternative policies." *Harvard Educational Review* 43 (November, 1973): 556–598.

35. McCall, G. "More thoughts on the Ik and anthroplopgy." *Current Anthropology* 16 (September, 1975):344–348.

36. McKinley, D.G. *Social Class and Family Life.* New York: Fress Press, 1964.

37. Marshall, D.S. "Sexual behavior on Mangaia," in *Human Sexual Behavior,* p. 153. Edited by D.S. Marshall and R.C. Suggs. Englewood Cliffs, N.J.: Prentice-Hall, 1971.

38. Murdock, G.P. *Social Structure.* New York: Macmillan, 1949.

39. Mussen, P. and Beytagh, L.A. "Industrialization, child-rearing practices, and children's personality," *Journal of Genetic Psychology* 115 (December, 1969):195–216.

40. Nash, J. "Death as a way of life: The increasing resort to homicide in a Maya Indian community." *American Anthropologist* 69 (October, 1967): 455–470.

41. Nuttall, E.V. and Nuttall, R.L. "The effects of size of family on parent-child relationships." *Proceedings of the Annual Convention of the American Psychological Association,* pp. 267–268, 1971.

42. Nye, I.F., Carlson, J., and Garrett, G. "Family size, interaction, affect, and stress." *Journal of Marriage and the Family* 32 (May, 1970):216–226.

43. Olsen, N.J. "Family structure and socialization patterns in Taiwan." *American Journal of Sociology* 79 (May, 1974):1395–1417.

44. Opler, M.E. "Themes as dynamic forces in culture," *American Journal of Sociology* 51 (November, 1946):198–206.

45. Otterbein, K.F. "The anthropology of war," in *Handbook of Social*

and Cultural Anthropology, pp. 923–958. Edited by J.J. Honigmann. Chicago, Ill.: Rand McNally, 1974.

46. Otterbein, C.S. and Otterbein, K.F. "Believers and beaters: A case study of supernatural beliefs and child rearing in the Bahama Islands." *American Anthropologist* 75 (November, 1973):1670–1681.

47. Parke, R.D. and Collmar, C.W. "Child abuse: An interdisciplinary review," in *Review of Child Development Research,* Vol. 5. Edited by E.M. Hetherington. Chicago, Ill.: University of Chicago Press, 1975.

48. Pearlin, L.I. *Class Context and Family Relations: A Cross-National Study.* Boston: Little, Brown, and Co., 1970.

49. Prescott, J.W. "Body pleasure and the origins of violence." *The Futurist* 9 (April, 1975):64–74.

50. Riches, D. "The Netsilik Eskimo: A special case of selective female infanticide." *Ethnology* 13 (October, 1974):351–361.

51. Rappaport, R.A. *Pigs for the Ancestors: Rituals in the Ecology of a New Guinea People.* New Haven: Yale University Press, 1968.

52. Russell, E.W. "Factors of human aggression: A cross-cultural factor analysis of characteristics related to warfare and crime." *Behavior Science Notes* 7 (July, 1972):275–312.

53. Sahlins, M.D. "The segmentary linage: An organization of predatory expansion." *American Anthropologist* 63 (April, 1961):322–337.

54. Schlegel, A. *Male Dominance and Female Autonomy: Domestic Authority in Matrilineal Societies.* New Haven: Hraf Press, 1972.

55. Singer, J.L. "The influence of violence portrayed in television or motion pictures upon overt aggressive behavior," in *The Control of Aggression and Violence,* pp. 19–56. Edited by J.L. Singer. New York: Academic Press, 1971.

56. Sipes, R.G. "War, sports, and aggression: An empirical test of two rival theories." *American Anthropologist* 75 (February, 1973):64–68.

57. Steinmetz, S.K. "Occupational environment in relation to physical punishment and dogmatism," in *Violence in the Family,* pp. 166–172. Edited by S.K. Steinmetz and M.A. Straus. New York: Dodd, Mead and Co., 1974.

58. Steinmetz, S.K. "Intrafamilial patterns of conflict resolution: United States and Canadian comparisons," paper presented at the annual meetings of the Society for the Study of Social Problems, 1974.

59. Steinmetz, S.K. and Straus, M.A., eds. *Violence in the Family.* New York: Harper and Row (Originally published by Dodd, Mead), 1974.

60. Straus, M.A. "Some social antecedents of physical punishment: A linkage theory interpretation." *Journal of Marriage and the Family* 33 (November, 1971):658–663.

61. Straus, M.A. "A general systems theory approach to a theory of violence between family members," *Social Science Information* 12 (June, 1973): 105–125.

62. Straus, M.A. "Leveling, civility, and violence in the family." *Journal of Marriage and the Family* 36 (February, 1974):13–29 (plus addendum in August 1974 issue).

63. Straus, M.A. "Cultural and social organization influences on violence between family members," in *Configurations: Biological and Cultural Factors in Sexuality and Family Life,* pp. 53–69. Edited by R. Price and D. Barrier. Lexington: Lexington Books, 1974.

64. Straus, M.A. "Sexual inequality, cultural norms, and wife-beating." *Victimology* 1(1, 1976):54–76.

65. Textor, R.B. *A Cross-Cultural Summary.* New Haven: Area Files Press, 1967.

66. Toby, J. "Violence and the masculine ideal: Some qualitative data," in *Patterns of Violence: The Annals of the American Academy of Political and Social Science,* pp. 20–27. Edited by M.E. Wolfgang. Philadelphia: American Academy of Political and Social Science, 1966.

67. Turnbull, C. *The Mountain People.* New York: Simon and Schuster, 1972.

68. Vayda, A.P. "Expansion and warfare among swidden agriculturalists." *American Anthropologist* 63 (April, 1961):346–358.

69. Weigert, A.J. and Thomas, D.L. "Family as a conditional universal." *Journal of Marriage and the Family* 33 (February, 1971):188–194.

70. Whiting, B.B. "Sex identity conflict and physical violence: A comparative study." *American Anthropologist* 67 (February, 1965):123–140.

71. Wilson, P.J. "More thoughts on the Ik and Anthropology." *Current Anthropology* 16 (September, 1975):343–344.

3

Child Abuse in the International Year of the Child

Lesli Taylor and
Eli H. Newberger

Children have been documented as victims of violence, neglect, abandonment, slavery, and murder since records of mankind have been kept.[25, 79, 85] Only within the past century has the notion developed that children have rights apart from those that adults choose to grant them. In 1959, the United Nations Declaration of the Rights of the Child stated, "The child shall be protected from all forms of neglect, cruelty and exploitation."[23]

The child-welfare movement began in the United States during the middle and late 19th century when the exploitation of children and adults during the Industrial Revolution led to undeniable signs of childhood suffering: homeless and starving, children wandered the streets. The sight of these children led, in turn, to concern for the moral growth of the children of the poor. Home was believed to be a haven for children and the setting where their spiritual development into upright and productive citizens should be nurtured.[40]

Not until the 1950's did the medical community begin systematically to note that many children were in fact harmed by their parents. Radiologists noted fractured bones associated with head injuries in infants and speculated that the injuries might have been inflicted by parents or other persons responsible for the children's care.

But it was the article that appeared in 1962 in the *Journal of the American Medical Association* by Professor C. Henry Kempe and his colleagues that coined the diagnosis, the battered-child syndrome. The article was written with the explicit intention of arousing public concern and spurring professional action for the protection of children.[51] This publication was associated with an editorial outcry in both professional and lay media, and it led directly to the promulgation by the United States Children's Bureau of a model statute for the reporting by physicians of victims of child abuse. By the middle 1960's, every state in the country had laws mandating the reporting of

Reprinted by permission from the *New England Journal of Medicine*. Vol. 301, pp. 1205–1212; 1979. Supported in part by a grant (#1TO1MH15517-01A2CD) from the National Institute of Mental Health.

This paper was prepared at the invitation of the International Year of the Child Secretariat, UNICEF Headquarters, New York.

battered children. Today, all professionals with responsibility for the care of children are obliged to report suspected cases of child abuse.

Other Western industrialized nations have involved agencies of the state in the protection of children in their homes. The countries where child abuse and neglect appear most visibly to be the targets of professional action are those where the organic or biologic sources of illness and death in children have largely been controlled.

With the celebration of the International Year of the Child, the rights of children to be free from maltreatment have again been recognized worldwide. As of May, 1979, the following countries had identified child abuse and neglect as worthy of special concern: Austria, Belgium, Bermuda, Ghana, Guyana, Hong Kong, India, Ireland, Liberia, Sudan, the United States, and Zambia. According to information supplied by the International Year of the Child Secretariat, many countries have also been involved in studies relating to the rights of the child. These include Barbados, Finland, France, the Federal Republic of Germany, the German Democratic Republic, Hungary, Indonesia, Nicaragua, Nepal, Poland, Senegal, and the Syrian Arab Republic.

Definition

There is no consensus among professionals about the definition of child abuse and neglect. There is controversy about whether the definition should be narrow or broad. The original paper on the battered-child syndrome by Professor Kempe and his colleagues described the syndrome as resulting from harmful acts by parents or foster parents.[51, 52] Here, the notion was of injuries inflicted on children; a concept of intent to harm the child was implicit.

A broadened definition, which is suitable for medical diagnosis but does not presuppose a desire to harm the child, is "an illness stemming from situations in his home setting which threaten a child's survival."[73]

Professor David Gil, whose book, *Violence Against Children,* was the first systematic study of case reports on child abuse, proposed yet a broader definition of child abuse in hearings before the United States Senate on what ultimately became legislation establishing a Center on Child Abuse in the Department of Health, Education, and Welfare. Gil described child abuse as "any act of commission or omission by individuals, institutions, or society as a whole and any conditions resulting from such acts or inaction, which deprive children of their equal rights and liberties and/or interfere with their optimal development, constitute by definition abusive or neglectful acts or conditions."[38]

Whether child abuse should be seen in terms of the plight of individual children or whether the problem should be recognized as an issue for society is the subject of vigorous, frequently rancorous debate. There are, furthermore, culturally accepted methods of childrearing that result in physical harm to a child. How these situations should be dealt with is by no means clear. The following examples drawn from several countries show the range of practices that may be considered child abuse. In America, a three-year-old boy was admitted to the hospital after being beaten by his father. Physical examination showed a broken arm and bruises all over the child's body. An operation performed after the child vomited blood revealed abdominal visceral injuries.[104] In Czechoslovakia, identical twins were isolated from human contact and treated cruelly by their stepmother from their 18th month until they were seven years old, resulting in subnormal intelligence, rudimentary speech, rickets, inability to walk, and terror of people and normal objects.[56] In Nigeria, a seven-year-old child died after being shot by an angry guardian. The child had a history of three previous hospitalizations for trauma.[76] Most people would agree that the aforementioned cases constitute child abuse. But what about the following cases, in which the intent to do harm is not apparent?

In Vietnam, a four-year-old child was forced to submit to the practice of Cao Gio ("scratch the wind"), or coin-rubbing, in which a child's oiled back is stroked with a coin until bruises appear, to help rid the body of "bad winds." It is unclear how painful or harmful this is to the child.[3,94] In America, a Little League baseball pitcher, eight years old, injured his elbow because he was pressured by his parents to excel in sports.[60,80,110] In Latin America, a folk remedy for depression of the soft spot on an infant's head (caida de mollera) prescribes holding the infant by the ankles while dipping the crown of his head into very hot water. This practice may cause both scalded skin and hemorrhage around the brain.[43]

These examples show the diversity of maltreatment of children and suggest some cultural practices and values associated with child abuse: corporal punishment, superstition and the concern that twin babies may be evil, the right of the parent to harm or destroy his offspring, the infliction of pain and injury as healing, and the traumatic consequences of competitive athletics. Each country has values and practices that may culminate in injury or suffering to children. In the industrialized world and especially in the United States, the dramatic manifestations have led to awareness and to a probing of the origins of child abuse and neglect. After initial recognition of the problem, more formalized professional and governmental action may follow.

Manifestations of Child Abuse

As described in the medical literature, the clinical signs of the battered-child syndrome include bruises, welts, lacerations, abdominal injuries, ocular damage, burns, and bone fractures. Skull fracture and bleeding around the lining of the brain have been frequently noted and reported.[2,15,100] Shaking an infant may cause injury to the child's neck, bleeding within the skull, and brain injury that may be associated with early death or with profound and continuing neurologic and psychologic disturbances.[16] Frequently, the diagnosis of severe child abuse is supported by the simultaneous presence of new injuries to bone and soft tissue and by signs of previous trauma, often detected on physical examination or on an x-ray film. Some victims of child abuse are found to have only recent injuries. Others, however, have such diverse symptoms of mistreatment as to give the impression of a long-standing pattern of abuse. This has led to expressions of concern that if action is not taken promptly, the consequences may be fatal.

Infanticide has a long history. Its persistence to the latter part of the 20th century may have to do with the same cultural and economic realities that appear to have been associated with the killing of infants in the past: the wish to destroy illegitimate offspring, the belief in ritual sacrifice, the desire to destroy defective babies, and the need to control population growth. In some cultures, the last born in a set of twins or triplets may be killed if the mother is feared to be unable to care for the child; if a mother dies in childbirth, her child may be buried alive with her.[82] A grim reminder of the relation between infanticide and economics is the practice recently reported in Thailand of buying a baby from unknowing parents, killing the child, and using the body to smuggle heroin.[105] It has been asserted that at one or another time every culture has practiced infanticide.[6,61,87,101,105] Infanticide has also been associated with unwanted births and with mothers' psychiatric problems after delivery.[4,86]

The syndrome called "failure to thrive" has been associated with the neglect of children. Here, the children fall below the third percentile for weight and height; their neurologic and psychologic growth has also slowed, and no signs of organic illness account for the deficiencies. Characteristically, children who fail to thrive show marked improvement when separated from their parents, either in the hospital or in foster homes.[29] Failure to thrive has frequently been described in families in which mothers cannot fulfill their children's emotional and nutritional needs. There may have been a failure to form an adequate mother-infant bond at birth or the mother may have serious psychiatric problems; the child, too, may have special qualities that inhibit expressions of normal nurturing by the parent.[10,32,111]

Failure to thrive can be distinguished from kwashiorkor and marasmus, which are nutritional disorders frequently found in developing countries.[106] Occasionally, a child may starve to death because of deliberate action or neglect by a parent.[1] It has been proposed that failure to thrive, neglect, and abuse form a continuum of symptoms, perhaps from the same causes.[54]

Neglect may be defined as a parent's failure to meet a child's needs for food, clothing, shelter, hygiene, medical care, education, or supervision. It is important to take into account the parent's economic ability to provide these items and thus the parent's intent when a child appears neglected.[7] Obviously, in many underdeveloped countries where poverty is rampant, people of all ages suffer for want of basic necessities. In these situations, a parent cannot be blamed for the child's symptoms, but action must still be taken to help the child.

Emotional or psychologic abuse of children is difficult to define. The psychologist James Garbarino has proposed the definition, "the willful destruction or significant impairment of the child's competence."[36]

The problems of sexual exploitation of children have received increasingly greater attention in the past five years, and Professor C. Henry Kempe has noted that we are now discovering sexual abuse, just as in the early 1960's we discovered child abuse. He defines sexual abuse as, "the involvement of dependent and developmentally immature children and adolescents in sexual activities that they do not fully comprehend, to which they are unable to give informed consent, or that violate social taboos of family roles."[50]

Cultural factors may also figure in the sexual abuse of children. In Muslim countries, children may be taken as brides, whereas in Western countries, sexual interaction between adults and children may be construed as a criminal act or as a symptom of psychologic disturbance. Incest and less traumatic and invasive sexual acts toward children have been blamed for various levels of physical and psychologic harm to the child.[9,26,77,91] Brandt and Tisza have proposed the concept of "the sexual misuse of children" to draw attention to the fact that normal and necessary physical relations between children and their parents or guardians can sometimes become more intense and sexual than society will tolerate.

A newly recognized form of child abuse is Munchausen's syndrome by proxy. Munchausen's syndrome is a psychiatric illness in which the patient creates a physical illness in order to gain attention and medical treatment. A case has been reported in the United States of a mother injecting fecal material into her daughter and, after widespread infection was diagnosed in the child, withholding antibiotics. This caused serious recurrent infections and several hospitalizations.[55] In England, a mother falsified her child's medical history and substituted contaminated urine samples for the child's own urine so that the child was admitted to the hospital on several occasions.[69] In these situations, the child is the unwitting victim of a serious psychiatric problem in the parent.

Causes of Child Abuse

Just as there are many symptoms of child abuse, there appear to be many causes. The child may have qualities that provoke abuse. He or she may be small at birth and difficult to care for.[46,53] It may be difficult for parents and child to form an emotional bond. The child may be hyperactive or precocious and thus demand a great deal from parents; physical handicaps or a mismatch in the child's and parent's temperaments may make it especially difficult to cope with the angry feelings that all parents have at one time or another. Mental retardation has been described in association with child abuse, although it may be difficult to determine whether violence against the victim preceded or succeeded the disability.[30] The parent may perceive the child as different or unusual in relation to other children; parents' perception of a child may be distorted if a child is unwanted, illegitimate, or adopted. [24,33]

Abusive parents have been characterized as immature and unable to see their children as children. They may think that a baby, for example, is crying just to make them angry. They may believe that a child should be toilet trained by the age of six months or that the child should be able to help cook and clean the house at the age of 18 months. When parents of abused children are interviewed, many indicate that they as children were abused themselves. They may know no other method of child rearing than violence. Drug and alcohol addiction and major mental illness have been described in relation to child abuse, but many parents who abuse their children are psychologically normal. They may have suffered recent serious stresses, such as the loss of a loved one or a recent move to an unfamiliar community. It has been asserted that psychologic analyses of child abuse are inadequate, and that the presence or absence of social supports and stresses may better explain the individual case and indicate the route to prevention.[37]

Families in which child abuse or neglect have occurred often appear to have suffered serious environmental stresses, such as crises in housing and in access to essential services and supports. These problems may be associated with less parental tolerance of children and with explosions of violence.[74] Child abuse may also be seen as a subset of a larger set of family problems involving violence, including abuse by one spouse of the other, violence among siblings, and attempts by children to harm their parents.[102]

Values of a society may influence methods of child rearing at home. The acceptance of corporal punishment in schools may encourage parents to use harsh discipline. In his article, "Controlling Child Abuse in America: An Effort Doomed to Failure," the distinguished American psychologist Edward Zigler contends that so long as corporal punishment is sanctioned, child abuse will be inevitable.[113] Many societies sanction violence as an acceptable method of controlling behavior and of solving conflicts.

Whether child abuse results from individual or social causes is the subject of much discussion in the literature on the problem. Although individual cases cry out for action on behalf of particular children, the prevention of child abuse must involve reassessing the values, practices, and realities of family life.

The Sequelae of Child Abuse

Child abuse may have far-reaching consequences. Both abuse and neglect of children have been described as causes of brain damage and mental retardation.[19,71] A child may be left with permanent physical deformities. There may be major emotional and psychologic consequences.[28,35,68] The only controlled follow-up study published to date, however, indicates that poverty may be as important as maltreatment in causing psychologic deficits in children.[27]

Concern has also been expressed about the long-term impact of child abuse. Violent juvenile delinquents have been described as having suffered or witnessed great amounts of violence in their lives.[13,64] It has been further proposed that victims of child abuse may become the abusers of the next generation.[99]

Current Problems in Dealing with Child Abuse

The great conflict in developing programs for the protection of children has to do with whether children have rights of their own. Article 17 of the International Covenant on Civil and Political Rights (United Nations, December 16, 1966) states, "No one shall be subjected to arbitrary or unlawful interference with their privacy, family, home. . . Everyone has the right to the protection of the law against such interference."[17] The privacy of the home, however, may make it difficult to fulfill the United Nations Declaration of the Rights of the Child: "The child shall be protected from all forms of neglect, cruelty and exploitation."[23]

In present practice, professional services aim to protect the child and simultaneously help the parents to understand their own problems. Most programs to protect children involve social workers who are trained in counseling parents. Often, homemaker and child-care services are offered to help allay the stresses that may make it difficult for a parent to care for a child.

Frequently, however, parents are reluctant to cooperate. In these situations, more intrusive and coercive actions may be taken. These actions sometimes involve juvenile, family, or criminal courts. Although the child may be separated from the parents, the action is usually justified in terms of providing the child and the parent with professional assistance. Often the parent is portrayed as "sick" and in need of treatment.[75] In the best present practice, professionals expert in child protection work together to provide coordinated medical, social, psychiatric, and child-development services to families in which children have been abused and neglected. Frequently, however, it is difficult for workers in separate institutions to collaborate in serving families with many problems. The past decade has seen the development in many places of interdisciplinary teams that work from different bases—hospitals or community social-service agencies, for example—and that provide many services to families whose children are reported as victims. Many social-welfare programs for victims of child abuse are crippled by too many cases for too few workers and a heavy emphasis on separating children from their parents.[72] Frequently, doctors ignore child abuse or resist dealing with other professionals because the problems are so emotionally distressing to them or because they do not have the time or interest to do more than care for a wound.[18,45,93]

Sometimes the cure for child abuse can be worse than the disease. Children have been reported often as victims of abuse and neglect in the foster homes in which they have been placed for protection.[57] Not only do professionals have to be trained to recognize child abuse and to treat the victims sensitively and humanely, but the agencies assigned by the state to care for the problems of abused and neglected children need to be staffed sufficiently; foster homes, when they are needed, must themselves be safe, nurturant, and well supervised.

Cross-Cultural Comparisons

Children are still seen as chattel in many countries. Some are forced to be beggars, and they may be mutilated to make them more effective at it.[34] Children are still used as soldiers, and they are often victims of wars that they did not choose to fight.[97] Child labor remains extensive throughout the world, with current estimates approaching 52 million children under the age of 15 years in the work force; 42 million of them work without pay.[31] In the practice of jeetah in India, children are sold to the parents' landlord, by whom they may be mistreated.[95]

Aggressiveness toward children appears to vary according to culture. German adults in one study were found to be more aggressive toward their children than were Danes or Italians.[5] Child rearing among the Alorese was consistently seen in another study to rely heavily on shaming and aversive discipline, and such methods were accepted within that culture by all adults.[88] A study in Ireland indicated that alcoholism among fathers may be linked to abuse of mothers and children, especially among the poor.[66] In one area on the Gulf of Guinea in West Africa, corporal punishment of children may include use of a switch or a whip, and cuts received from a beating may be made more painful by the rubbing of pepper into the wounds and into other sensitive parts of the child's body.[63]

Corporal punishment is a time-honored and socially sanctioned form of discipline. Forty-six states in America permit corporal punishment in the schools, as do Australia, Barbados, Canada, Ireland, New Zealand, South Africa, Swaziland, Trinidad, Tobago, and the United Kingdom.[44,103]

Most Western and Eastern European countries, including the Communist bloc countries, have outlawed corporal punishment in the schools. Sweden has made corporal punishment at the hands of the parents illegal as well; Norway plans to do the same. Although the law is unenforceable for practical purposes, its effect is intended to be pedagogic and to change social attitudes.[107] Corporal punishment is frowned on as a method of discipline in Japan, modern China, and the Soviet Union.[11,41,98] If the person administering corporal punishment in a school wants to humiliate or harm a child as well as to maintain order, serious injuries may occur.[20,39]

Some socially sanctioned customs may hurt a child, and whether these practices should be labeled child abuse depends on the observer. Such practices as scarification, binding of the skull or feet, and a variety of painful pubertal initiation rites may do lasting harm.[8,58,96] Male and female circumcision have been called abusive, although they clearly have religious and cultural meaning that make them widespread practices.[42,65] In the light of current concerns about the right of children to be protected from cruelty, it is anticipated that these practices will be reevaluated.

Child abuse has been identified as a problem in many countries: Australia, Canada, East Africa, India, Malaysia, New Zealand, and South Africa, as well as most Western European countries.[14,21,22,47,48,70,78] Child abuse is said not to exist or to be very rare in modern China, Russia, Poland, and Japan.[11,49,67,89,112] Whether or not a country acknowledges the problem depends on its local definition and priority. For many, the problem would be too embarrassing to admit; for some, serious violence against children may seem normal.

Some societies have values and standards of child rearing that appear to lower the likelihood of child abuse. The birth of a child in the Papago Indian culture brings great prestige to the parents and may mark their transition to full adult status; the child is valued and cherished.[88] In Russia, children are held in high esteem by all adults; strangers may show concern for children as if the children were their own.[11] In societies in which extended families are the norm, young parents are relieved from constant care of the child. Children also learn as they grow up about the care of other children, and they may learn at an early age to deal with the problems of parenthood by other than violent means.[109] Child care in China, Russia, and Israel is provided by the state. In some cultures in China, a custom called "doing the month" results in a 30-day period in which a mother and her infant are apart. There would seem to be little opportunity for the establishment of normal mother-child attachment.[81] Yet this Western concept of bonding, the lack of which has recently been suggested to have predictive value, may be of limited usefulness in a cross-cultural comparison. There is apparently no child abuse in cultures in which this separation of mother and child takes place. China's state policy strongly favors late marriage and the spacing of children.[98] Family supports that may reduce the prevalence of child abuse and neglect in the United Kingdom, France, Israel, and Poland include universal health-care programs for mother and child.[49]

In cultures in which infants are given great amounts of physical affection and adult sexual proscriptions are few, there appear to be fewer violent acts by adults toward children.[83,84]

Suggestions for Action

The first step in coming to terms with child abuse is to recognize it. When child abuse is defined, assumptions about the care of children and about injurious but socially accepted practices will come under scrutiny. Only then can legislation and policy be formulated to deal with child abuse and neglect.

Many areas of contention remain. Who has the ultimate responsibility for children—their parents or the state? Should parents retain power over the life and death of their offspring? Is childbearing an inalienable right, or should governments determine who can be parents? These questions go beyond the cultural position of children, to the political status of individuals and families. They demonstrate the extent to which defining child abuse and elaborating a social policy to deal with it are linked to the country's values and social and political structures. The following recommendations for action are intended to stimulate discussion regarding the prevention and treatment of child abuse at several levels: community, government, and worldwide.

Community Action

At the community level, both families with children and professionals who care for children need to be aware of the problem of child abuse. Schools of medicine, law, and social work should include child abuse in their curriculums and encourage professional work to prevent and treat the problem. It must be understood, however, that professionals alone will not solve the problem of child abuse.

Personnel in hospitals with pediatric departments frequently see injured children and are in a position to identify child abuse and neglect. Educating the staff and forming links to other supportive services in the community will permit identification of individual cases and help ensure that the children return to safe, nurturant homes.

Plans to prevent child abuse at the local level must take into account the socioeconomic status of the community and the institutions that serve parents and children. In less affluent communities, it may be possible only to educate parents about the development of children and nonviolent means of raising them. Violence against children can be outlawed in public schools.

In more affluent communities, such family supports as child-care centers and health programs for mothers and children that include counseling and help for marital problems will go far to prevent child abuse. The mobility of families throughout the world in response to war, rural poverty, and the attraction of jobs in the cities may isolate parents and children and rupture the ties to extended family and friends that make it possible to tolerate the demands of children.[59,92] Attention must be paid to the needs of families in transition; the special problems of political refugees, victims of famine and war, and linguistically isolated parents and children must be acknowledged forthrightly and compassionately by all who care for children.

Hospitals can revise routines to help make childbirth a favorable experience. Breast feeding can be encouraged and made more socially acceptable by professionals educating the public about its benefits.

Churches and other community organizations can organize programs to support families. Housing programs can be planned to avoid the segregation of people by age, race, and social class, which leads to isolation, frustration, and stress.[12]

Local services today strive to keep children with their parents, even after abuse has occurred. Keeping the home together requires the development of professional skills and the availability of such supports as child care and homemaker services; it also requires a commitment to maintain the integrity of the family even in the face of serious adversity and the presence of great risk.

Government Action

Nearly all governments now have laws that address the welfare of children, if not statutes requiring the reporting of child abuse and neglect. To prevent child abuse, several initiatives are possible at the government level. A "family-impact statement" has been proposed as a counterpart to the environmental-impact statement required for all major government-funded programs in the United States. Rigmor von Euler of Sweden's Save the Children Federation has suggested the appointment of a children's ombudsman who could act on the behalf of any child.[108]

Corporal punishment by parents and by institutions that deal with children can be reduced through policies, laws, and vigorous efforts to educate parents and teachers in other methods of socializing children. Recent studies of the impact of violence in the media on children's behavior suggest a need to reduce the extent to which violence is presented as a legitimate way of resolving conflict.[62] Government regulation may be required, although respect for individual civil liberties and freedom of the press must be considered in the formulation of national policy.

In countries where child abuse has been studied systematically, there appears to be a prevalence of unwanted children in the reports. The development of more liberal family-planning programs should make it possible for parents to have children only when they want them and feel prepared to care for them.

The association of child abuse with poverty suggests that one of the most important government initiatives to control child abuse will be to make available to young families certain basic necessities, including adequate housing, employment, and health care. Countries with universal health-care systems in which the programs for maternal and infant care include regular visits by a nurse at certain points in infancy appear to prevent child abuse more effectively.[103] Child abuse is not inevitable. Governments can have an important role in its perpetuation or its eradication. Governments can encourage the study of child abuse. This task will entail compiling an analysis of case reports, evaluating and guiding preventive and therapeutic efforts, promoting communication between social scientists and clinical workers, and funding pertinent research on child development and the family.

World Action

Although all will agree that children represent the future of the world, it is clear that throughout most of the world the welfare of children lags behind as a priority. Of particular concern is the extent to which defense budgets outstrip allocations for services to children and families. Implements of destruction seem everywhere to be more important than supports to ease the suffering of the young. It is encouraging to note that the Socialist Republic of Romania has reduced its military expenditures by $42 million, approximately one fifth of its 1977 defense budget. Part of this money will be used to increase state allowances for children.[90]

An important worldwide action that will help to prevent child abuse is the international exchange of information through conferences and journals, already under way during the International Year of the Child. A better understanding of how children are reared in other cultures will help us to understand how we can make life better for children in our own.

Though much will be done to further the rights of children during the International Year of the Child, this effort will have to be sustained and increased in the years to come. At a time when enough weaponry exists to destroy the population of the world, we have everything to gain by rearing the next generation in peace.

References

1. Adelson, L. "Homicide by starvation: The nutritional variant of the 'battered child.' " *JAMA* 186 (November, 1963):458–460.

2. Altman, D.H. and Smith, R.L. "Unrecognized trauma in infants and children." *Journal of Bone and Joint Surgeon* (Am) 42 (April, 1960): 407–413.

3. Anh, N. " 'Pseudo-battered child' syndrome." *JAMA* 236 (November, 1976):2288.

4. Arboleda-Florez, J. "Infanticide: Some medicolegal considerations." *Canadian Psychiatric Association Journal* 20 (February, 1975):55–60.

5. Bellak, L. and Antell, M. "An intercultural study of aggressive behavior on children's playgrounds." *American Journal of Orthopsychiatry* 44 (July, 1974):503–511.

6. Blum, R. and Blum, E. "Birth, abortion and death," in *Health and Healing in Rural Greece,* pp. 71–80. Stanford, Calif.: Stanford University Press, 1965.

7. Bourne, R. "Child abuse and neglect: An overview," in *Critical Perspectives on Child Abuse,* pp. 1–14. Edited by R. Bourne and E.H. Newberger. Lexington, Mass.: Lexington Books, 1979.

8. Brain, J.L. "Sex, incest, and death: Initiation rites reconsidered." *Current Anthropology* 18 (June, 1977):191–208.

9. Brant, R.S. and Tisza, V.B. "The sexually misused child." *American Journal of Orthopsychiatry* 47 (January, 1977):80–90.

10. Brazelton, T.B. "The parent-infant attachment." *Clinical Obstetrics and Gynecology* 19 (June, 1976):373–389.

11. Bronfenbrenner, U. *Two Worlds of Childhood: US and USSR.* New York: Russel Sage Foundation, 1970.

12. Bronfenbrenner, U. "Reality and research in the ecology of human development," in *Child Abuse and Violence,* pp. 230–273. Edited by D. Gil. New York: American Medical Society Press, 1979.

13. Button, A. "Some antecedents of felonious behavior." *Journal of Clinical Child Psychology* 2(3, 1973):35–37.

14. Bwibo, N.O. "Battered child syndrome." *East Africa Medical Journal* 49 (November, 1972):934–938.

15. Caffey, J. "Multiple fractures in the long bones of infants suffering from chronic subdural hematoma." *American Journal of Roentgenology* 56 (1946):163–173.

16. Caffey, J. "On the theory and practice of shaking infants: Its potential residual effects of permanent brain damage and mental retardation." *American Journal of Diseases in Children* 124 (August, 1972):161–169.

17. Caulfield, B.A. "Legal questions raised by privacy of families and the treatment of child abuse and neglect." *Child Abuse and Neglect* 1(1, 1977): 159–166.

18. Chang, A., et al. "Child abuse and neglect: Physician's knowledge, attitudes and experience." *American Journal of Public Health* 66 (December, 1976):1199–1201.

19. Chase, H.P. and Martin, H.P. "Undernutrition and child develop-

ment." *New England Journal of Medicine* 282 (April, 1970):933–939.

20. Comer, J. "Spanking." *New York Times,* 29 December 1975, p. 25.

21. Dawe, K.E. "Maltreated children at home and overseas." *Australian Paediatric Journal* 9 (August, 1973):177–184.

22. Dawe, K.E. "Child abuse in Nova Scotia." *Australian Paediatric Journal* 9 (December, 1973):294–296.

23. Declaration of the Rights of the Child by the United Nations General Assembly, November 20, 1959.

24. de Lissovoy, V. "Toward the definition of 'abuse provoking child.'" *Child Abuse and Neglect* 3(1, 1979):341–350.

25. DeMause, I., ed. *The History of Childhood.* New York: Psychohistory Press, 1974.

26. Densen-Gerber, J. and Hutchinson, S.F. "Sexual and commercial exploitation of children: Legislative response and treatment challenges." *Child Abuse and Neglect* 3(1, 1979):61–66.

27. Elmer, E. "A follow-up study of traumatized children." *Pediatrics* 59 (February, 1977):273–279.

28. Elmer, E. and Gregg, G.S. "Developmental characteristics of abused children." *Pediatrics* 40 (October, 1967):596–602.

29. English, P.C. "Failure to thrive without organic reason." *Pediatric Annals* 7 (November, 1978):774–781.

30. Eppler, M. and Brown, G. "Child abuse and neglect: Preventable causes of mental retardation." *Child Abuse and Neglect* 1(2–4, 1977): 309–313.

31. "52 million children are labourers." *IYC Report* (Newsletter of the International Year of the Child.) New York: United Nations, 1978, p. 2.

32. Fischhoff, J., Whitten, C.F. and Pettit, M.G. "A psychiatric study of mothers of infants with growth failure secondary to maternal deprivation." *Journal of Pediatrics* 79 (August, 1971):209–215.

33. Freidrich, W.N. and Boriskin, J.A. "The role of the child in abuse: A review of the literature." *American Journal of Orthopsychiatry* 46 (October, 1976):580–590.

34. Gage, N. "To many boys, Istanbul streets are home." *New York Times,* 28 June 1979, sec. A, p. 3.

35. Galdston, R. "Observations on children who have been physically abused and their parents." *American Journal of Psychiatry* 122 (October, 1965):440–443.

36. Garbarino, J. "The elusive crime of emotional abuse." *Child Abuse and Neglect* 3(1, 1979):89–99.

37. Gelles, R.J. "Child abuse as psychopathology: A sociological critique and reformulation." *American Journal of Orthopsychiatry* 43 (July, 1973):611–621.

38. Gil, D.G. "Unraveling child abuse." *American Journal of Orthopsychiatry* 45 (April, 1975):346–356.

39. Gilmartin, B. "The case against spanking." *Human Behavior* 8(1979):18–23.

40. Goldstein, H. "Child labor in America's history." *Journal of Clinical Child Psychology* 5 (Winter, 1976):47–50.

41. Goode, W.J. "Force and violence in the family." *Journal of Marriage and the Family* 33 (November, 1971):624–636.

42. Grimes, D.A. "Routine circumcision of the newborn infant: A reappraisal." *American Journal of Obstetrics and Gynecology* 130 (January, 1978):125–129.

43. Guarnaschelli, J. " 'Fallen fontanelle' (caida de mollera): A variant of the battered child syndrome." *JAMA* 222 (December, 1972):1545–1546.

44. Hechinger, F.M. "Many schools still rely on the 'hickory stick.' " *New York Times,* 24 July 1979, sec. C, p. 4.

45. Helfer, R. "Why most physicians don't get involved in child abuse cases and what to do about it." *Children Today* 4 (May–June, 1975):28–32.

46. Hunter, R.S. et al. "Antecedents of child abuse and neglect in premature infants: A prospective study in a newborn intensive care unit." *Pediatrics* 61 (April, 1978):629–635.

47. Hwang, W. "Battered child syndrome in a Malaysian hospital." *Medical Journal of Malaysia* 28(4, 1974):239–243.

48. Irwin, C. "The establishment of a child abuse unit in a children's hospital." *South African Medical Journal* 49 (July, 1975): 1142–1146.

49. Kamerman, S. "Eight countries: Cross-national perspectives on child abuse and neglect." *Children Today* 4 (May–June, 1975):34–37.

50. Kempe, C.H. "Child abuse—the pediatrician's role in child advocacy and preventative pediatrics." *American Journal of Diseases of Children* 132 (March, 1978):255–260.

51. Kempe, C.H. et al. "The battered child syndrome." *Journal of the American Medical Association* 181 (July, 1962):17–24.

52. Kempe, C.H. and Helfer, R.E., eds. *Helping the Battered Child and His Family.* Philadelphia: Lippincott, 1972.

53. Klein, M. and Stern, L. "Low birth weight and the battered child syndrome." *American Journal of Diseases of Children* 122 (July, 1971): 15–18.

54. Koel, B.S. "Failure to thrive and fatal injury as a continuum." *American Journal of Diseases in Children* 118 (October, 1969):565–567.

55. Kohl, S., Pickering, L.K. and Dupree, E. "Child abuse presenting as immunodeficiency disease." *Journal of Pediatrics* 93 (September, 1978):466–468.

56. Koluchova, J. "Severe depression in twins: A case study." *Journal of Child Psychology and Psychiatry* 13(2, 1972):107–114.

57. Knitzer, J., Allen, M.L. and McGowan, B. *Children Without Homes.* Washington, D.C.: Children's Defense Fund, 1979.

58. Korbin, J. "Anthropological contributions to the study of child abuse." *Child Abuse and Neglect* 1(1, 1977):7–24.

59. Korbin, J. "A cross-cultural perspective on the role of the community in child abuse and neglect." *Child Abuse and Neglect* 3(1, 1979):9–18.

60. Kranepool, E. "Youth and sports: Beware of pressures to be a star and the obsession to win." *New York Times,* 11 September 1977, sec. 5, p. 2.

61. Langer, W.L. "Infanticide: A historical survey." *History of Childhood Quarterly* 1 (Winter, 1974):353–365.

62. Lefkowitz, M.M. et al. *Growing Up to Be Violent.* New York: Pergamon Press, 1977.

63. LeVine, R.A. "Childrearing in sub-Saharan Africa." *Bulletin of the Menninger Clinic* 27 (September, 1963):245–256.

64. Lewis, D.O. et al. "Violent juvenile delinquents: Psychiatric, neurologic, and psychologic and abuse factors." *Journal of the American Academy of Child Psychiatry* 18 (Spring, 1979):307–319.

65. Lowenstein, L.F. "Attitudes and attitude differences to female genital mutilation in the Sudan: Is there a change on the horizon?" *Social Science and Medicine* 12 (September, 1978):417–421.

66. Lukianowicz, N. "Incest: I: Paternal Incest: II: Other types of incest." *British Journal of Psychiatry* 120 (March, 1972):301–313.

67. Lythcott, G.I. "Some observations on pediatric health in the People's Republic of China." *Man and Medicine* 2(1977):133–147.

68. Martin, H.P. et al. "The development of abused children." *Advances in Pediatrics* 21(1974):25–73.

69. Meadow, R. "Munchausen syndrome by proxy: The hinterland of child abuse." *Lancet* 2 (August, 1977):343–345.

70. Monaghan, S.M. and Couper-Smartt, J. "Experience of an anticipatory management programme for potential child abuse and neglect." *Child Abuse and Neglect* 1(1, 1977):63–69.

71. Morse, C.W. et al. "A three-year follow-up study of abused and neglected children." *American Journal of Diseases of Children* 120 (November, 1970):439–446.

72. Nagi, S. *Child Maltreatment in the United States: A Challenge to Social Institutions.* New York: Columbia University Press, 1977.

73. Newberger, E.H. et al. "Reducing the literal and human cost of child abuse: Impact of a new hospital management system." *Pediatrics* 51 (May, 1973):840–848.

74. Newberger, E.H. et al. "Pediatric social illness: Toward an etiologic classification." *Pediatrics* 60 (August, 1977):178–185.

75. Newberger, E.H. and Bourne, R. "The medicalization and legalization of child abuse." *American Journal of Orthopsychiatry* 48 (October, 1978):593–607.

76. Nwako, F. "Child abuse syndrome in Nigeria." *International Surgeon* 59 (Nov.–Dec., 1974):613–615.

77. Parker, G. "Incest." *Medical Journal of Australia* 1 (March, 1974): 488–490.

78. Paul, S.D. "Recognition of the entity 'the battered child syndrome' in India." *Indian Journal of Pediatrics* 39 (February, 1972):58–62.

79. Pfohl, S.J. "The discovery of child abuse." *Social Problems* 24 (February, 1977):310–323.

80. Pigott, R. "Youth and sports: Beware of child abuse." *New York Times,* 11 September 1977, sec. 5, p. 2.

81. Pillsbury, B.L. " 'Doing the month': Confinement and convalescense of Chinese women after childbirth." *Social Science and Medicine* 12 (January, 1978):11–12.

82. Pintak, L. "Ken Messerman, US missionary in war-torn Rhodesia." *People Magazine* (June, 1979):33.

83. Prescott, J.W. "Body pleasure and the origins of violence." *Futurist* 9 (April, 1975):64–74.

84. Prescott, J. "Deprivation of physical affection as a primary process in the development of physical violence: A comparative and cross-cultural perspective." In *Child Abuse and Violence,* pp. 66–137. Edited by D. Gil. New York: American Medical Society Press, 1979.

85. Radbill, S. "A history of child abuse and infanticide," in *The Battered Child,* pp. 3–21. Edited by R.E. Helfer and C.H. Kempe. Chicago: University of Chicago Press, 1968.

86. Resnick, P.J. "Child murder by parents: A psychiatric review of filicide." *American Journal of Psychiatry* 126 (September, 1969):325–334.

87. Riches, D. "The Netsilik Eskimo: A special case of selective female infanticide." *Ethnology* 13 (October, 1974):351–361.

88. Rohner, R. *They Love Me, They Love Me Not: A Worldwide Study of the Effects of Parental Acceptance and Rejection.* New York: Human Relations Area Files Press, 1975, pp. 97–163.

89. Rollins, N. *Child Psychiatry in the Soviet Union: Preliminary Observations.* Cambridge, Mass.: Harvard University Press, 1972, pp. 25–41.

90. "Romania cuts arms budget." *IYC Report* (Newsletter of the International Year of the Child.) New York: United Nations, 1979, p. 1.

91. Rutanen, E. "Research in Finland in 1973." *Psychiatria Fennica* (Yearbook of the Psychiatric Clinic of the Helsinki Central Hospital.) Helsinki: Helsinki Central Hospital, 1973, pp. 17–22.

92. Safilios-Rothschild, C. "Trends in the family: A cross-cultural perspective." *Children Today* 7 (March–April, 1978):38–43.

93. Sanders, R.W. "Resistance to dealing with parents of battered children." *Pediatrics* 50 (December, 1972):853–857.

94. Sandler, A.P. and Haynes, V. "Nonaccidental trauma and medical folk belief: A case of cupping." *Pediatrics* 61 (June, 1978):921–922.

95. Sathyavathi, K. "Suicide among children in Bangalore." *Indian Journal of Pediatrics* 42 (June, 1975):149–157.

96. Schegel, A. and Barry, H. III. "Adolescent initiation ceremonies: A cross-cultural code." *Ethnology* 18 (April, 1979):199–210.

97. Shopper, M. "Children and war," in *Child Abuse and Violence,* pp. 586–595. Edited by D. Gil. New York: American Medical Society Press, 1979.

98. Sidel, R. *Women and Child Care in China.* Baltimore: Penguin Books, 1972.

99. Silver, L.B. et al. "Does violence breed violence? Contributions from a study of the child abuse syndrome." *American Journal of Psychiatry* 126 (September, 1969):404–407.

100. Silverman, F.N. "The roetgen manifestations of unrecognized skeletal trauma in infants." *American Journal of Roentgenology* 69(1953):413–427.

101. Solomon, T. "History and demography of child abuse." *Pediatrics* 51 (April, 1973):773–776.

102. Steinmetz, S.K. and Straus, M.A. *Violence in the Family.* New York: Harper and Row, 1974.

103. "The last? resort." *Newsletter of the Committee to End Violence against the Next Generation* (March–June, 1979).

104. Touloukian, R.J. "Abdominal visceral injury in battered children." *Pediatrics* 42 (October, 1968):642–646.

105. "Trafficking in death." *Far Eastern Economic Review* 103 (April, 1979):5.

106. Vaughan, V.C. and McKay, R.J., eds. *Nelson's Textbook on Pediatrics.* Philadelphia: Saunders, 1977, pp. 183–186.

107. Vinocur, J. "Swedes shum Norse agage." *New York Times,* 4 April 1979, sec. A, p. 7.

108. von Euler, E. "The child and violence." *Save the Children Federation of Stockholm,* 4 July 1978.

109. Weisner, T.S. and Gallimore, R. "My brother's keeper: Child and sibling caretaking." *Current Anthropology* 18 (June, 1977):169–190.

110. Wheatly, G. "Introduction: Pediatric aspects of sports medicine." *Pediatric Annals* 7 (November, 1978):663–665.

111. Wolff, P.H. "Mother-infant interactions in the first year." *New England Journal of Medicine* 295 (October, 1976):999–1001.

112. Wray, J.D. "Child care in the People's Republic of China: 1973." *Pediatrics* 55 (April, 1975):539–550.

113. Zigler, E. "Controlling child abuse in America: An effort doomed to failure," in *Critical Perspectives on Child Abuse,* pp. 171–213. Edited by R. Bourne and E.H. Newberger. Lexington, Mass.: Lexington Books, 1979.

4

Eight Countries: Cross-National Perspectives on Child Abuse and Neglect

Sheila B. Kamerman

In the spring of 1972, a cross-national research study covering eight countries was launched at Columbia University School of Social Work.[1] The study was undertaken in response to a widespread interest in policy, program and administrative issues in general social services in the United States, and the assumption was that one way to develop new perspectives on what exists in this nation would be to study what is being done in other countries. We would then compare the provision of social services across the countries and analyze the relationship of such provision to political, economic, social and cultural contexts. The seven countries involved, in addition to the United States, are Canada, France, West Germany, Israel, Poland, the United Kingdom and Yugoslavia.

The study deals with the somewhat amorphous group of services which remain after income maintenance, health, psychiatry, education, housing and employment programs are separated out. The major objective of the study is to determine whether a "personal" or "general" social service system is emerging; that is, whether what is left after one removes those systems specified above can be identified as a distinctive, cohesive cluster of services. And if that is so, what might its boundaries, characteristics, tasks and problems be?

Operating within time and budget constraints, the study sampled the "personal" social service domains in each country by focusing on six topics or fields of particular interest in the United States. One of these fields is the focus of this article: "Early Identification and Intervention Into the Problem of Child Abuse and/or Neglect."[2]

To avoid ambiguities deriving from language problems and to assure data comparability, the study stressed operational definitions and descriptive reporting, in accord with a standard data collection instrument. For the problem of child abuse/neglect, the following major questions were posed:

- What is meant by "child abuse and neglect"? How are these terms defined? Is abuse and neglect one problem or two? How extensive is (or are) the problem(s)?
- What is the nature and extent of existing provision—legislation, policies, programs—at all governmental levels and in both public and voluntary

Reprinted with permission from Sheila B. Kamerman, "Eight Countries: Cross-national perspectives on child abuse and neglect." *Children Today* 4(3):34–37, 1975.

sectors? Which are the major agencies and organizations concerned with the problem?

• What devices—provisions—are there for locating and identifying abused/neglected children?

• What kinds of programs have been developed to deal with the problem of child abuse/neglect? How extensive are these? Whom do they serve? Who staffs them? What do they cost?

• What is the nature of relevant research? What, if anything, is known about the relative effectiveness of different interventions—for prevention, for prediction, for treatment? In general, what is known and what knowledge is being sought?

• What are the major issues currently identified by experts in the field?

In each participating country, data were assembled and analyzed by leading researchers, natives of the countries studied. Reports were written and service models described for various parts of each country. In addition, one or more local jurisdictions were selected in each nation for more detailed description and analysis, with the focus placed here on how services were being delivered.

The following represents a preliminary summary and analysis of the responses obtained to these questions, for the study is still in process. Some of the material is still being translated and our foreign colleagues have yet to review these generalizations. What is presented now is certainly not a comprehensive analysis, nor does it begin to include all the material assembled. It does, however, highlight trends, issues and relevant developments.

What Is Meant By Child Abuse And Neglect?

Social problems are only perceived as problems—and defined as such—in the context of specified societal values, and these values are transitory in time or place. Thus, perception of child abuse and neglect differs in our various countries. Some of the nations in the study recognize child abuse as a separate, identifiable, distinctive problem but assume that to the extent the problem exists, adequate response is being provided within the existing child protective (child welfare) service. In other countries it is perceived as such a minor problem that no special attention is required. Yugoslavia, for example, does not even separate out the problem of child neglect from the general issue of "pre-delinquency." Another country, Poland, recognizes the existence of child abuse but its reported incidence is considered to be slight. Provision for dealing with the problem is within the scope of general child protective services; however, these are said to need expansion and improvement.

However, the five other countries in our study, like the United States, have been increasingly aware of child abuse/neglect. And all are struggling with similar problems, perhaps the most fundamental of which is that of definition. Canada and the United Kingdom come closest to the United States in their current preoccupations and in their beginning efforts in making distinctions along the continuum between abuse and neglect. Both countries stress the concept of a continuum, although the British and Canadians use the expression "cruelty, ill treatment, neglect," with abuse implying the most serious kind of injury to a child. In Israel, France and Germany there is still discussion as to whether there is any valid reason for separating out or highlighting "abuse" as a distinctive entity. The position taken in these countries is that concern should be directed more appropriately towards all maltreated children.

As part of the phenomenon of child abuse, all five countries (that is all studied except Poland and Yugoslavia) have begun to take notice of the "battered child syndrome" and have followed the United States literature on the subject with great interest. Yet here too the lack of any precise, standardized, operational definition is pervasive. For example, a recent national report issued in Canada defined child battering in words that will be familiar to many of us: "the intentional non-accidental use of physical force by the caretaker aimed at hurting, injuring or destroying the child." [3] Note here that what is being identified is one narrowly defined problem, focused on the intentional behavior of the perpetrators, not on the consequences to the child. Discussion of this point in Canada highlighted a problem for all countries: how does one distinguish "intentional" from "non-intentional" behavior?

Clearly, such questions as whether or not child abuse/neglect is a matter of public concern, how abuse/neglect is defined, whether reporting laws exist and for whom reporting is mandatory, whether accurate records are kept and the extent to which laws are implemented all affect figures of reported incidence. Researchers in all countries agree, therefore, that there are no firm data on incidence of child abuse/neglect. Existing studies indicate that as definition and laws change, and registries are set up, the count becomes higher. In Germany as in the United States, debate exists as to whether indications of increased incidence are real or only reflect changes in reporting. (And if they are real, the debate continues, does this reflect the inevitable consequences of increased industrialization or something else?) In Canada, there is some discussion as to whether or not the whole preoccupation with incidence is not misplaced, since the real issue is meeting the needs of children in need generally.

Legislation, Policies and Programs

Canada, France, Germany, Israel, Poland and the United Kingdom—like the United States—all have traditional child protective legislation dealing with the problems of neglected children. Identification of child abuse as the "tip of the iceberg" of this larger problem has emerged only gradually in some of these countries. Inevitably, special provision is limited.

Apart from the United States, only Canada (seven out of 10 provinces) has legislative provision specifically addressing the problem of child abuse. Both public and voluntary (or more accurately, quasi-public) agencies are involved in implementing these laws. Three provinces have central registries for keeping records of abuse or suspected incidents of abuse.

In the United Kingdom, official recognition of the problem of child abuse has not given rise to any new legislation as yet, but it has led to a series of communications to local authorities and health service workers from central government departments concerned with child care and health services. The major thrust of these communications is that child abuse is only part of the problem of neglect and ill treatment of children and that staff should be particularly sensitive to the potential for injury of "children at risk" or where abuse is suspected.

Although there is nothing like a central registry in the United Kingdom, several local social service authorities (public social service agencies) have established registries as a part of special programs and/or units. Some of these are hospital based or jointly administered by both health and social service systems. Responsibility for provision is located primarily in the public sector, although some voluntary organizations (in particular, the National Society for the Prevention of Cruelty to Children (NSPCC) are also active.

Our British colleague reports current trends as follows: "In so far as the concern over battered children is leading to any pressure for new legislation, it is to tighten up present procedures by making what is presently permissive —e.g., reporting and keeping of registers—prescriptive. But what are primarily being sought are more energetic and efficient ways of administering the present child protection laws. . . ."[4]

There has been particularly heated debate throughout 1974 in the United Kingdom as a result of several publicly reported, dramatic incidents of child abuse—and one major formal governmental inquiry.[5] Questions have been raised in Parliament; legislation has been introduced, if not passed; and numerous articles have appeared in the popular press and professional journals. Social workers have been accused of ineptness and incompetence in handling cases at risk and they have faced the dilemma involved in balancing concepts of protection and freedom.

In Israel also, no special legislation exists regarding child abuse. In fact, there is still debate as to whether incidents of abuse are sufficient to warrant a governmental response distinct from the overall child welfare and child protective service. What new initiatives have been taken there have been under the aegis of the voluntary sector, led primarily by pediatricians.

Similarly, in France a small group of pediatricians has expressed concern about the battered baby syndrome. However, theoretically all children—battered, abused, neglected, ill treated, deprived or otherwise—are covered by the overall child welfare program. Furthermore, the French stress the need for a more comprehensive and integrated family policy (social policy for families) and tend to frown on discrete, specialized programs.

Identifying the Children

It is here that several of the countries in our study reveal a particularly interesting pattern. Except for Canada, no other country studied has found it necessary to develop the kind of special programs we have in the United States for identifying such children. The United Kingdom, France, Israel, and Poland all have universal maternal and child health programs of varying types, in which all children are seen regularly from infancy on, thus facilitating, although not guaranteeing, identification of such cases. In the United Kingdom, the health visiting program involves mandatory health screening of infants soon after birth and regular at-home visits by specially trained visiting nurses in all homes, especially those thought of as potentially at risk.[6] Once children attend school, health care is integrated into that system and regular examinations are routine.

Israel has a national network of universal, free or low-fee maternal and child health clinics, used extensively by almost all and providing the basis for an excellent across-the-board case-finding system. France, too, has a universal maternal and child health service which includes compulsory medical examinations. If a mother does not bring her child for any of the regularly scheduled examinations, the family social worker is notified and visits at home to determine the problem. This is not to say that the social worker's task is easy. Where the worker takes action which eventually leads to a child's removal from home, one result may be neighborhood hostility. The social worker may be so stigmatized that she may be unable to work effectively in that neighborhood again. On the other hand, a similar consequence may occur if the worker does not follow through by removing a child when the neighborhood perceives clear and present danger.

In Poland, where child abuse is not yet defined as a separate problem, the potential for identification of neglected children is good because there is a universal health service and mandatory reporting requirements for doctors with reference to "anything unusual." Thus, the doctors in the child health system identify cases and social workers follow up on them.

Child Abuse/Neglect Programs

Where there have been special initiatives directed towards intervention with regard to this problem, the pattern has been clear and consistent. All agree that primary prevention requires good social policy for children—adequate family income, health services and housing and special efforts at improving and enhancing family life, parenting, and child socialization. For case finding (location and identification) of abused children, a universal and extensive maternal and child health service is clearly the predominant and preferred approach. Other special programs are not needed where this pattern exists. With regard to treatment programs, although there is nothing unique in any of these countries and nothing which would surprise Americans working in this field, the approaches reported include:

• The recognized need for multi-disciplinary and multiple interventions including but not limited to emergency short term facilities for child placement and care, homemaker services, day care and therapeutic groups.

• The recognized need for extended follow-up and continuity of care and the expectation that some form of care may be necessary for a very long time. For example, the French consider six months an absolute minimum period for follow-up after an incident requiring intervention, assuming that the child is not removed from the home or at least not for an extended period of time. The average follow-up period there is three to four years and eight to 10 years is not uncommon.

• The need for what the British call a "case manager" (and what we have termed a "case integrator") to assume responsibility for continuity of care to the family. This role or function ensures accountability by coordinating, meshing or integrating all services needed by the family at one time and/or over time. It is this function that is described repeatedly by professionals in all countries as the cornerstone of any treatment plan—and thus of any special program.

In general, special programs for the treatment of abused children are not seen as needed, although Canada and Israel each has at least one program that is comparable to the model developed by Kempe and Helfer[7]—that of a hospital-based intervention and treatment program. Adequate resources and the growing emphasis on the essential role of the case manager in service provision generally—to coordinate services and staff from several other disciplines—are stressed. All agree that close relationships between health, legal and social services are essential. In the United Kingdom, the emphasis is on implementing this within the local personal social service system, in order to avoid further fragmentation.

Relevant Research

Formal research and evaluation studies among the seven other countries studied are even more limited than in the United States and, as we know, research is in its incipient stages here. As already indicated, there is no consensus about the nature of the phenomenon and its extent, or about the effectiveness of alternative methods of intervention. Therefore, no provision for reporting, evaluating or providing feedback can be agreed on.

Major Issues Addressed

Clearly the major debate relates to whether or not child abuse represents a phenomenon distinct from maltreatment of children generally and whether it warrants special policies and programs. The consensus seems to be that there is one overall entity; that there are variations within it encompassing a continuum of severity of consequences for children; that where the danger may be greatest for children—in instances of physical abuse—there should be some priority for intervention. However, there continues to be difficulty in specifying and standardizing the criteria delineating the parameters of these priority cases. In this context, the movement in most other countries seems to be one of improving provisions for care of *all* children and families, rather than developing additional, separate, specialized or categorical programs. In short, one can hardly talk about adequate service for these children without including the essentials outlined earlier; health, income maintenance, housing, day care, family planning, residential treatment, homemakers, local social service delivery and good social policy for children generally.

Where the debate touches on the need for specialized programs, the issue seems to be the inadequacies in existing child welfare programs. A consequence of this may be initiatives by pediatricians or social workers, responding to public outrage at specific and horrendous incidents of abuse. As in the United States, inadequacy of resources (money, staff, training, knowledge), fragmentation of services and provision, lack of accountability, and interdisciplinary professional and organizational conflicts are the most frequent criticisms of traditional programs. The new approaches are designed to reduce these problems by stressing improved social policy and provision for children generally and, at the level of service delivery, by concentrating on multiple interventions, multidisciplinary efforts implemented over time, and coordination of all provision by an individual specifically identified as the professional-in-charge of the case: the case manager.

The developments described represent an interesting cross-national phenomenon: an illustration of what might be termed "cultural diffusion" of a problem and/or of a concept. Although concern with what may or may not be a distinctive and growing phenomenon related to highly industrialized societies emerged first in the United States—and still seems greatest here —similar developments have emerged in Canada and the United Kingdom and, to a lesser extent, in Israel, France and Germany.

The issues discussed in most of the countries participating in our study are similar. In several countries discussion about the existence of the problem and the need for social intervention has focused on the issue of individual rights. Thus, for a long time, society relaxed when children were with their parents and in households because it was assumed that parents had absolute rights and complete authority over their children. Recently, more attention has been paid to children's rights and the interest in abuse and neglect seems to be part of this trend. In some countries, child abuse/neglect is defined as a social class problem—a problem of the poor. Yet no research documents this and many would agree that reported incidence may be greater among the poor because it is they who are more likely to be exposed to the public authorities who do the counting.

Finally, the current stress on child abuse rather than on the problem of children who are in need and who need help has raised important and basic questions. Among these are:

• Is this concern with child abuse as a separate and distinct problem a critique of existing child welfare systems and programs? And does the delineation of child abuse as a separate problem represent an effort at eliminating the inadequacies of general child welfare programs?

• Can this current stress on child abuse be a "stalking horse"—a way of taking the lead and taking initiative in a movement to expand resources and provision for child welfare programs generally?

• Are these current developments in danger of becoming a "red herring" —a way to divert attention from the need for more basic social policy and social provision?

• Is child abuse a phenomenon with none of these functions but a validly separate and distinctive entity requiring unique societal response?

It is too soon to attempt definitive answers.

Notes

1. Basic support for the study is provided through the Social and Rehabilitation Service, HEW (Office of Research and Demonstration, Sec. 110 SSA). The studies in Israel, Poland and Yugoslavia are funded under P.L. 480. Research in Canada is financed entirely by the Canadian Council on Social Development. Supplementary funds or "in kind" aid have been provided by various institutions and agencies in the United Kingdom, France and Germany. A grant from OCD supports the preparation of those materials for the United States report relating to the children's field and a contract with NIMH covers preparation of analyses and reports related to its interests.

2. The other five topics are: Day Care and Related Preschool Programs; Institutions and Community-Based Residential Arrangements for Delinquent and Neglected Children; Access Services in Family Planning and Abortion

Services; Community Care for the Aged; and Social Service Delivery at the Local Level.

3. *Report of the National Ad Hoc Advisory Committee on Child Battering,* Ottawa, 1973.

4. Rodgers, Barbara, "Location and Help for Young Children Who are Abused, Neglected, and Battered," Report prepared for Cross-National Studies of Social Service Systems, covering this topic in the United Kingdom.

5. *Report of the Committee of Inquiry into the Care and Supervision Provided in Relation to Maria Colwell,* Department of Health and Social Security, London, HMSO, 1974.

6. For a more extensive description of what the Health Visitor does, see "Health Visiting in England," Alfred J. Kahn and Sheila B. Kamerman, *Beyond the Poor Law: Social Services for All,* Philadelphia: Temple University Press (in press).

7. Kempe, C. Henry and Helfer, Ray E., eds., *Helping the Battered Child and His Family,* Philadelphia: J.B. Lippincott Co., 1972.

5

Physical Punishment of Children and Wifebeating in Cross-Cultural Perspective

David Levinson

This paper reports the results of a worldwide cross-cultural study of the relationship between wifebeating and the physical punishment of children. The notion that wifebeating and physical punishment of children may be linked is derived from the Straus[6,8] feedback model of wifebeating. Straus argues that "family socialization through violence" is one of a number of sociocultural factors leading to frequent wifebeating. Family socialization through violence involves children observing parental violence, violence among siblings, the encouragement of violent behavior in boys, and physical punishment of children. Straus suggests a snowball effect, with family socialization through violence leading to high rates of wifebeating, and high rates of wifebeating maintaining other forms of violence within the family.

In this paper we report a test of the hypothesized linkage between wifebeating and physical punishment of children with a sample composed of 60 small-scale and folk societies. A small-scale society is a distinct cultural unit with no indigenous written language. A folk society is a society whose members share a common cultural tradition, produce at least 50% of their own food, and are under the political control of a larger nation-state.

This paper is divided into three sections. In the first section we discuss the methods used to test the wifebeating-physical punishment hypothesis. In section two we present the results of the test. And in the final section we discuss the implications of the test results.

Methodology

The sample for this study is the Human Relations Area Files Probability Sample Files (PSF) composed of 60 well-described small-scale and folk societies representing all major cultural regions of the world.[2,5] All of the data used in this study were collected from ethnographic reports included in the

Reprinted with permission from D. Levinson, "Physical punishment of children and wifebeating in cross-cultural perspective," in *Child Abuse and Neglect* 5(4), Pergamon Press, Ltd., 1981.

Human Relations Area Files data archive. The HRAF data archive is a cross-referenced, cross-indexed collection of ethnographic reports describing the ways of life of some 315 different ethnic, national, and subcultural groups from all geographical regions of the world. Because of missing data for either the wifebeating or physical punishment variable, the sample size is reduced to 46 societies.

Wifebeating is defined as the physical assault of a woman by her husband and is measured on a four-point scale:

4. Common—wifebeating occurs in all or nearly all households in the society.
3. Frequent—wifebeating occurs in a majority but not nearly all households in the society.
2. Infrequent—wifebeating occurs in a minority of households in the society.
1. Rare—wifebeating does not occur or occurs in only a small minority of households in the society.

Physical punishment is defined as the use of physical force by caretakers to discipline, motivate, or punish a child or infant and is also measured on a four-point scale:

4. Common—physical punishment is used more often than other socialization techniques such as scolding or withholding of privileges.
3. Frequent—physical punishment is used as often as other socialization techniques.
2. Infrequent—physical punishment is used less often than other socialization techniques.
1. Rare—physical punishment is used less often than other socialization techniques.

Results

The descriptive results of this study indicate that wifebeating occurs more often than the physical punishment of children and infants. In the 46 societies sampled, wifebeating is common in 17%, frequent in 24%, infrequent in 39%, and rare in 19%. Physical punishment is common in only 4%, frequent in 22%, infrequent in 37%, and rare in 37% of the societies sampled. This finding supports Barry and Paxon[1] who report also that harsh disciplinary techniques tend to be absent in small-scale societies.

As regards the hypothesized relationship between wifebeating and physical punishment, statistical analysis supports such a relationship. The *gamma* coefficient of .34 ($p < .05$) displayed in table 5–1 indicates that the use of physi-

Table 5-1

Relationship between Physical Punishment and Wifebeating

| Wifebeating | Physical Punishment | | | |
	Rare	Infrequent	Frequent	Common
Rare	Andamans Copper Eskimo Ifugao Iroquois Ona Thailand	Rural Irish Hopi Trobrianders		
Infrequent	Kanuri Lapps Lau Mataco Tucano	Klamath Masai Ojibwa Pygmies Santal Taiwan Tikopia Tzeltal	Ashanti Cagaba Garo Pawnee Wolof	
Frequent	Bororo Iban Tarahumara	Kapauku Korea Kurd Toradja	Azande Dogon Somali	Amhara
Common	Chukchee Tlingit Yanoama	Aymara Hausa	Ganda Truk	Serbs

Gamma = .34, $p < .05$

cal punishment as a socialization technique with children is associated with frequent wifebeating. However, if we examine the distribution of the societies listed in table 5-1, we find that the relationship is more complex than is suggested by this one correlation coefficient alone. The distribution of the societies in the top half of the table (columns 1-4, rows 1-2) shows a strong relationship between rare or infrequent physical punishment of children and rare or infrequent wifebeating. Of the 27 societies listed in the top half of table 5-1, 22 follow the low punishment-low wifebeating pattern. However, the distribution of the societies in the lower half of the table (columns 1-4, rows 3-4) shows a muddled relationship between frequent physical punishment and wifebeating. In fact, the distribution in the lower half runs opposite Straus' prediction, with 12 societies showing a low punishment-high wifebeating pattern and only 7 showing the predicted high punishment-high wifebeating pattern. Straus, of course, suggests that frequent wifebeating will be associated with frequent physical punishment.

While this analysis supports Straus' hypothesis in general terms, it shows, more specifically, at a societal level that rare or infrequent physical punishment of children is associated with rare or infrequent wifebeating,[9] while frequent or common wifebeating is unrelated to the frequency with which physical punishment is used as a socialization technique.[5]

Implications

This brief study has two important implications. First, it shows that there are many cultures in the world where caretakers rely on physical punishment of children as a socialization technique far less often than in the United States, where 90% of parents use physical punishment.[6] This finding may be the result of two factors. First, the large number of societies included in the sample with extended family households.[3,4,7] In accord with this general pattern, 21 of the 34 societies in this study which report rare or infrequent physical punishment are societies with extended or polygynous family households. The extended or polygynous family household—low physical punishment linkage most likely reflects the presence of alternative caretakers in the household who share child rearing responsibilities. Second, the inclusion in the sample of a number of hunting and gathering societies with nuclear family households such as the Copper Eskimo or Ona. In these type of societies, too, children are rarely treated harshly.[7]

Third, while this paper provides only partial support for Straus' wifebeating-physical punishment hypothesis,[8] it more strongly supports his claim that one way to control wifebeating is to control the physical punishment of children.[8] This analysis shows that in societies where physical punishment is relatively unimportant as a socialization technique, wifebeating is far more likely to be absent than present. Thus, while wifebeating and physical punishment of children are not linked in a causal sense, they do seem to be linked in terms of prevention or control of violence in the family.

References

1. Barry, H. III and Paxon, L.M. "Infancy and early childhood: Cross-cultural codes, 2." *Ethnology* 10 (October, 1971):466–509.

2. Lagace, R.O. "The HRAF probability sample: Retrospective and prospect." *Behavior Science Research* 14 (July, 1979):211–229.

3. Levinson, D. "Population density in cross-cultural perspective." *American Ethnologist* 6 (November, 1979):742–751.

4. Minturn, L. and Lambert, W. *Mothers of Six Cultures: Antecedents of Child Rearing.* New York: John Wiley, 1964.

5. Naroll, R. "The proposed HRAF probability sample." *Behavior Science Notes* 2 (April, 1967):70–80.

6. Owens, D.M. and Straus, M.A. "The social structure of violence in childhood and approval of violence as an adult." *Aggressive Behavior* 1(3, 1975):193–211.

7. Rohner, R.P. *They Love Me, They Love Me Not.* New Haven: HRAF Press, 1975.

8. Straus, M.A. "A sociological perspective on the prevention and treatment of wifebeating," in *Battered Women: A Psychological Study of Domestic Violence,* pp. 194–238. Edited by Maria Roy. New York: Van Nostrand, 1977.

9. Straus, M.A. "Wife beating: How common and why?" *Victimology: An International Journal* 2(3/4, 1977–78):433–458.

**Part II
Child Abuse**

Introduction to Part II

The study of child maltreatment has been markedly ethnocentric, ignoring non-Western conceptions of abuse and neglect. The chapters presented in this part were selected to represent diverse geographical areas and to emphasize alternative concepts of child maltreatment.

Chapter 6, by Smith and Hanson, is from England, and chapter 7, by Oates, Davis, and Ryan, is from Australia. Both investigations examine possible causal associations with child abuse and select quite similar variables for study. Both chapters use the same methodological techniques. In both England and Australia, children and their parents who were identified as abuse cases in major hospitals are compared to children and their parents admitted to hospitals for causes other than domestic violence. Both research groups focus upon mother–child interaction by collecting data on difficulties with pregnancy, obstetric complications, and perinatal and neonatal experiences. Although these chapters approach the phenomenon of child abuse in a similar manner, however, they reach markedly different conclusions. Smith and Hanson conclude that pregnancy, obstetric, and perinatal or neonatal problems are not the primary causes of abuse. Rather, abusive incidents are the result of mothers, because of personality disorders such as neuroticism, perceiving their children as being more difficult to handle than other children. Statistically, abused children in the England study were no different than nonabused children in numbers of wakeful nights, degree of excitability, waking time, bed time, fatigue during the day, and poor appetite.

Oates, Davis, and Ryan, on the other hand, find that abusive Australian mothers perceived pregnancy as being more displeasing than nonabusive mothers, because of higher incidences of prematurity, obstetric complications, and neonatal problems. The researchers also examined a variety of other sociopsychological factors. They conclude that parents' unrealistic expectations of children, few social outlets, few separations from children, and problems associated with finances, housing, domestic friction, and poor health increased the likelihood of abusive incidences. In the Australian study, abuse is not seen as a result of personality disorders within the parent, but rather as the result of stressful social–psychological situations. Oates, Davis, and Ryan conclude that even "normal" parents can be abusers when faced with difficult childbirth experiences, unmet expectations, little social support, and problems resulting from everyday living.

Chapter 8, by Bhattacharyya, provides yet another explanation for child maltreatment. Bhattacharyya's article on child abuse in India is a classic application of social-disorganization theory. Abuse is defined as a broad phenomenon, resulting not from inadequate parent–child interaction but from an impoverished and changing society. Developing nations, in the past thought to have little experience with child abuse, are today becoming more aware of incidents of maltreatment. Bhattacharyya attributes this possible increase of abuse to the disorganization of traditional tribal ways of life. The modernization of developing countries changes the demands placed on the family and other institutions, which are often unable to meet these changing demands.

134 Battered Children: A Medical and Psychological Study

Selwyn M. Smith and
Ruth Hanson

Introduction

Growing awareness of violence to infants dates from 1946, when Caffey[4] described the association between subdural haematomata and fractures of the long bones in young children. The recognition almost a decade later that such injuries could be inflicted by parents[61] and the coining of the emotive term "battered child syndrome"[24] stirred doctors in America to recognize the alarming frequency with which such children had mistakenly been regarded as accidentally injured. Interest was aroused in England after case reports[15] in 1963 and the British Paediatric Association's warning memorandum[2] in 1966, which helped define the problem and offered guide lines for treatment.

Despite clinical descriptions of battered children[1,14,19,24,34,58] and their parents[29,48,50] there has been no previous comprehensive and controlled study which has included both medical and psychological assessments. Because the correct diagnosis is often missed and doctors are still unsuspecting,[56] this paper reports birth abnormalities, age, sex, types and degree of injury and their sequelae, and other important factors in 134 battered children.

Patients and Methods

Over two years 134 battered infants and children aged under 5 years and their parents were studied in detail. Fifty-three children who were admitted to the hospital as emergencies other than on account of accident or trauma acted as a control group. The mothers' ages, areas of origin, and consultants referring were the same in both groups.

Procedure.—All parents were seen as soon as possible after their child's admission. The general health and behaviour of the child and his siblings were recorded by standardized psychiatric and psychological interview.[48,49]

Reprinted with permission from the *British Medical Journal* 3 (September), S.A. Smith and R. Hanson, "134 battered children: A medical and psychological study," 1974, pp. 666–670.

The medical notes were examined and the extent of the injuries recorded. All survivors were photographed and underwent full blood counts and skeletal surveys. Birth weights were recorded from maternity hospital notes. Eighty-four family doctors were asked to examine their records and 48 replied. The rest of the children had no doctor. The subscales (locomotor development, personal-social behaviour, hearing and speech, hand-eye co-ordination, and performance) on the Griffiths' Mental Development Scale[16] were measured in all children whose physical condition did not obviously entail brain damage.

Results

Sex and Age.—Sixty-eight patients were boys and 66 (49%) were girls, and 110 were under 2 years (mean age 18.5 months). Emergency admissions to Birmingham Children's Hospital were significantly younger than non-emergency admissions ($x^2=79.30$; D.F.=4; P<0.001). Battered children were significantly younger than all other emergency admissions to the same hospital during 1971 ($x^2=9.5$; D.F.=4; P<0.05).

Bruises, Burns, and Scalds.—Thirty-eight children presented with conditions other than injuries. One-hundred-and-ten had bruises, most often on the

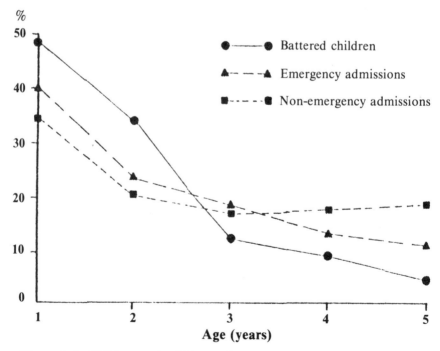

Figure 6-1. Children under 5 Years of Age Admitted to Birmingham's Children's Hospital.

head (75 cases) and thighs (45). Twenty-three had burns or scalds; in nine the buttocks and in six the lower limbs were affected, and injuries were most commonly caused by hot liquids or a metal stove. Cigarette burns occurred in two cases. Children with burns or scalds were older (mean age 24.8 months) than the remainder of the sample (t=2.35; P<0.05).

Fractures.—Forty-two children had recent or old fractures. The sites were skull (37 cases), humerus (19), radius and ulna (18), femur (17), tibia and fibula (17), other sites (28). Of those with burns 11 also had a fracture

Intracranial and Intraocular Haemorrhages.—Forty-seven children had an intracranial haemorrhage—subdural in 30 cases, subarachnoid in nine, and cerebral in eight. Of these 15 had no skull fractures and seven no head bruises. Of the total sample eight had ocular damage in the form of intraocular haemorrhages, exudates, papilloedema, or retinal detachments.

Seriousness of Injury

Twenty-one children died, 20 had serious injuries resulting in permanent damage, 62 had serious injuries but no apparent permanent damage, and 31 had superficial injuries.

Fifty-nine children had to stay in hospital for up to one week, 16 for 2–4 weeks, and seven for five weeks or more. Forty-eight remained in hospital for non-medical reasons for at least one extra week and seven stayed for at least five weeks.

Six dead children compared with 25 live children had a sibling who had been battered. Seven dead children compared with 65 of the rest had been battered more than once. Neither difference was significant. Twelve parents were convicted of either murder or manslaughter. In nine cases the coroner reached an "open verdict," and these parents were not prosecuted.

Comparison With Control Children

Abilities of Children.—Altogether 87 battered children were tested for mental development. Of these, 36 (27% of sample) had recovered from head injury (though the results of four cases were excluded because of serious congenital defects) and 51 (38%) had no injury other than bruising. Forty-one (31%) were untestable because of permanent damage and six (5%) were unavailable for testing. The mean general quotients on the Griffiths scale were 89 for battered and 97 for control children (t=2.79; P<0.01). Excluding those who recovered from their head injuries the contrast between battered children and controls was of smaller significance (t=2.03; P<0.05). Mean general quotients for battered children with head injuries from which they had clinically recovered and those without any head injuries were 87 and 90 respectively. Battered children

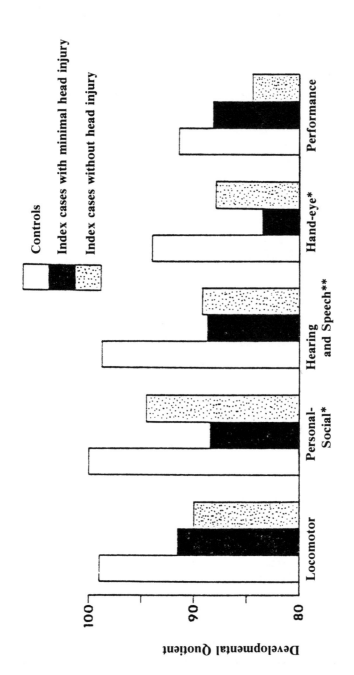

Figure 6–2. Developmental Quotients on Griffiths Scale.

Notes: Cases with relevant congenital defects were excluded from each group.

*Differences between controls and index cases with head injury are significant at 0.05 level.

**Differences between controls and index cases with head injury and between controls and index cases without head injury tested after head injury scored significantly lower than controls on personal-social, hearing and speech, and hand-eye co-ordination scales. There was no significant difference between battered children who had no head injuries and controls on the personal-social or hand-eye scales; only hearing and speech quotients were significantly lower for this subgroup of the battered sample. The mean developmental quotients of battered children of low birth weight was 73 and of those with failure to thrive 78.

Physical Neglect and Failure to Thrive.—Twenty-two battered children (16%) compared with one control (2%) were physically neglected on admission ($x^2=6.51$; D.F.=1; P<0.05), and 23 (17%) battered children compared with one (2%) control had previously been in hospital with failure to thrive ($x^2=6.62$; D.F.=1; P=0.01). Among the battered children failure to thrive occurred in 11 (50%) of the neglected children and 11 (10%) of the remainder ($x^2=17.64$; D.F.=1; P<0.001).

Birth Weight.—Of the battered children born in hospital 58 had normal birth weights, eight weighed between 2,000 and 2,500 g, and 11 weighed less than 2,000 g. The occurrence of low birth weight among the different social classes is shown in table 6-1 and compared with national norms.[10,57] In both upper and lower social classes the prevalence of low birth weight among the battered sample born in hospital was four times greater than the national rate.

Number of Deceased Siblings.—Ten battered children had a deceased sibling. Four of these had died under "suspicious" circumstances. In two cases more than one sibling had died. None of the controls had a deceased sibling.

Congenital Defects.—Altogether 7.46% (10) of the battered children had serious congenital defects as compared with 1.75% of the general population.[3] There were two cases each of spina bifida, hydrocephalus, and encephalocele and one each of Hirschsprung's disease, coeliac disease, congenital spherocytosis, and congenital dislocation of the hip. A further eight children had minor congenital abnormalities.

Precipitants.—Eighty mothers and 63 fathers initially denied inflicting injury but gave no adequate explanation of it, and 13 mothers and six fathers

Table 6-1

Percentage of Low Birth Weight Babies (2,500 g) according to Social Class in Three Studies

Social Class	Drillien	Present Study	National Survey of Health and Development
I and II	3.3		
III	5.9	24	5.6
IV and V	7.6	24	

Table 6-2
**Comparison between Behavior at Home of Battered Children
and Control Children**

	Battered Children		Controls		Significance	
	No.	%	No.	%	x^2	P
Wakeful at night (½/hr or longer)	11/23	9	11/51	22	4.12	<0.05
Excitable or lively	76/25	61	40/51	78	4.26	<0.05
Tired during day	49/124	39	31/51	61	5.76	<0.05
Rose 5-7 a.m.	38/123	31	16/51	31	0.01	N.S.
Went to bed 9-12 p.m.	30/123	24	15/51	29	0.25	N.S.
Poor appetite	15/124	12	7/51	14	0.00	N.S.
Crying a problem	39/107	36	4/48	8	11.69	<0.001

later changed their initial account into an adequate explanation of the injury. Battering incidents occurred equally in the morning (35 cases) and late afternoon (36). Thirty-one incidents occurred in the evening. Only five parents reported they battered the child late at night. Among mothers 16 had had a confinement less than three months previously, 56 between three and 12 months previously, and 62 more than 12 months before the battering incident.

Behavior of Child and Neuroticism among Mothers.—Battered children were significantly less wakeful at night, excitable or lively, or tired during the day than the controls (table 6-2). No significant differences were found in time of rising or going to bed or poor appetite. One child who failed to thrive was considered by its mother to have a feeding problem compared with 14 of those who did thrive. The difference was not significant. Forty (30%) mothers of battered children compared with five (9%) control mothers considered the child difficult ($x^2=8.40$; D.F.=1; P<0.01). Of the 40 mothers 30 (75%) were neurotic whereas only 29 (31%) of those who did not find their children difficult were ($x^2=16.21$; D.F.=1; P<0.001). Thirty-six (27%) mothers of battered children compared with four (8%) control mothers described their other children as difficult ($x^2=14.12$; D.F.=1; P<0.001). More (39; 29%) mothers of battered children—of whom 27 (69%) were neurotic—than control mothers (4; 8%) said crying, clinging, or whining behaviour was a severe problem ($x^2=11.49$; D.F.=1; P<0.001). Fewer of the mothers who did not find such behaviour a problem were neurotic—only 29 (31%) ($x^2=7.51$; D.F.=1; P<0.01).

Delay in Attending Hospital and Previous Contact with General Practitioners.—The parents of 82 battered children attended the hospital casualty department at least 24 hours after injury occurred. Eleven children with serious injuries (including some who later died from their injuries) were also presented after similar delay. According to the family doctor's reports no parent had made unnecessary visits. According to their own reports 113 had rarely or never consulted their general practitioner before battering their child.

Discussion

Some maintain that more boys than girls are battered,[13,29,46] but, along with others,[11,41] we have found equal numbers of both sexes. Several authors[25,43,45,46] suggest that younger children are particularly at risk. We have found that emergency admissions tend to be younger even if not battered. Nevertheless, battered children were significantly younger than other emergency admissions. Furthermore, most children were under 2 years of age and many had been previously battered, supporting suggestions that "any injury other than a road traffic accident to a child under 2 must be considered to be an instance of the battered baby syndrome."[56]

Our results confirm those of others who have shown that battered children have a multiplicity of injuries in various stages of healing.[11,24,58] Vague accounts—"must have knocked his head against the cot," "fell off the bed," "bruises easily,"—were offered as initial explanations by parents. In no case was a bleeding disorder detected. Bruising to the head or cheek, a black eye without gross bruising of the forehead, a "purple ear," or fading bruises of the ear and surrounding scalp were prominent features, supporting those who rate the head as an important site of trauma.[5,46]

Over a third of the children had an intracranial haemorrhage (usually subdural); many of these had no associated skull fractures, and 15% had no head bruising but showed instead minimal finger and thumb mark bruises on the trunk and arms. These children had been shaken violently, supporting Guthkelch's suggestions that repeated acceleration/deceleration (whiplash injury) rather than direct violence accounts for intracranial bleeding.[17] Diagnostic confusion also arose in those children with ocular damage. Here our findings concur with others who have concluded that physical maltreatment must be strongly considered when intraocular haemorrhages, with or without an associated subdural effusion, occur.

Burning

Though bruises, fractures, subdural haematoma, and malnutrition are being increasingly recognized as stigmata of baby battering little emphasis has been placed on child abuse by burning. Our finding that nearly one-fifth had serious burns or scalds and that such children were significantly older then the remainder of the sample supports suggestions that many incidents of child abuse by burning pass for accidents.[51] The importance of skeletal surveys (repeated two weeks later if negative) was shown by the fact that nearly half also had fractures. Cigarette burns were not common but burning of the buttocks or perineum by placing the child on a hot metal surface was a particularly striking feature—a finding also observed by Vesterdal.[55]

One-third of dead children had been battered previously and they had familiar injuries.[53,58] Most fatal injuries resulted from a single act of parental violence. A third had a sibling who had also been maltreated, and in 9% of cases the sibling had died—some under suspicious circumstances. These considerations should caution against the over-optimistic belief that only one child in a family is affected and emphasize the importance of considering care orders on siblings.

Adelson[1] and Emery[12] suggest that some "accidental" cases and "cot deaths" may be the results of parental assault. Sudden infant deaths are characterized by a long delay between the child last being seen alive and the discovery of death, illegitimacy, and low birth weight. Poor use of welfare services, poor living conditions, marital disharmony, and poor work records characterize the parents of such children.[39] Baby batterers share all these adversities.[49] Furthermore, half the sample of dead children were "discovered" after a delay of 24 hours or longer.

Mortality rates for children subjected to wilful violence vary among different series—less than 2%,[46] 3%,[14] 11%,[24] 25–30%,[20] and 55%.[55] Among our cases, after excluding cases where the parents had gone to prison, the rate was 8%—similar to that of Kempe[24] and Cooper.[7] Other series in this country have found higher rates.[18,33] The commonest cause of death in 0-4-year-olds are birth injuries, infections, and congenital abnormalities. Apart from "accidents," battering in Birmingham in 1971 ranked next above motor vehicle accidents as a cause of death.[6] But unless medical personnel overcome their reluctance to record a diagnosis of "battered child syndrome" [23] statistics will underestimate the problem. National statistics are also hampered; in five of our patients who died in Birmingham in 1971 the coroner reached an "open verdict." Thus none appeared in the Registrar General's figures[38] for "homicides and injuries purposely inflicted" in 1971.

Neurological and Intellectual Impairment

Our findings support those of others[20,31] who showed that battering often results in permanent neurological impairment. Spasticity, paraplegia, blindness, and other neurological sequelae that required long term rehabilitation developed in 15% of our cases. One child developed West's syndrome (infantile spasms, subnormality, hypsarrhythymia) after violent shaking.

Our findings also show that battering leads to developmental retardation. Abnormality of social responsiveness and visuomotor co-ordination were found in those children who had suffered only slight head injuries. Such behavior was, therefore, probably due to damage of the central nervous system and not to gazing silently and fixatedly out of mistrust.[36] Because the capacity for showing mistrust develops slowly in early childhood[42] observations of frozen watchfulness in young babies may be misinterpretations. In older children immobility can be a normal reaction to a new experience such as admission to hospital.[42] Children in our sample were tested after adaptation to hospital, and only one child behaved mistrustfully throughout testing.

Regardless of head injury, language retardation was found in our sample. This has also been observed by Martin.[31]

Thirty-eight per cent of the sample were without head injury or neurological damage, but their overall ability was also significantly lower than that of the controls. This may have been due to previous head trauma or genetic endowment.[48] Parental neglect may result in congenitally defective babies of low birth weight who fail to thrive.[8] Lower developmental quotients were obtained by children having such handicaps. Only 22 battered children were without brain damage, head injury, low birth weight, or failure to thrive.

Considering that most parents offer no adequate explanation of the injury and that in about half the patients with cerebral palsy and mental deficiency attending pediatric outpatient departments no adequate cause is identified[30] the possibility that battering is responsible for a sizeable proportion needs further exploration.

The possibility that childhood marasmus represents an associated form of rejection should be strongly considered.[47,52] A significant proportion of our sample had been previously admitted to hospital because of failure to thrive and were physically neglected, supporting the suggestion that maltreatment of children is a spectrum ranging from infanticide to nutritional and emotional deprivation.[28,31,43,45] It is established that lack of calorie intake and deprivation of maternal affection[44] may impair growth and curtail intellectual development.[60]

A quarter of battered children born in hospital had low birth weights. This figure falls to 15% if we assume that babies born at home were of normal weight and compares with 5-7% in the general population.[3,8,57] Several authors[14,45,46] have asserted that low birth weight babies are particularly at risk from battering, and others[26,27] have interpreted this as failure of bonding due to separating the mother from her child during the neonatal period. Many low birth weight babies in our own and other series[14,27,45,46] may, however, be simply explained as reflecting those maternal characteristics that predispose to delivery of low birth weight babies—low social class, youthful and single status, and rejecting attitudes during pregnancy.[8,10] All these characteristics were prevalent in our sample.[49] Newson has pointed out that responsiveness to a baby is not a simple matter of biological neces-sity but a general characteristic shared by many people who are not moth-ers.[35] Furthermore, unfavourable mother-child relationships are related to undesirable maternal attitudes long before the neonatal period[9] and to per-sonality abnormality.[37] Considering also that only a few babies weighed under 2,000 g at birth or required long-term separation from the mother it is unrealistic to expect that increased or improved maternal child contact after confinement[26,27] will substantially reduce the risk of subsequent battering.

Mother's Obstetric History

No support was found for suggestions that difficulties during pregnancy, labour, or after birth[43,46,50] are responsible. Most mothers had normal confinements and only a few babies were battered during the post-partum period. Indeed, many mothers had longstanding emotional and personality problems[48] and displayed rejecting attitudes towards their children irre-spective of puerperal factors.[49]

Possibly some children are particularly at risk and unwittingly invite physical abuse from their parents.[32] Failure to take account of the fact that child-parent I.Q. correlations are low before the age of 3 years[22] and failure to use well validated tests such as the Griffiths developmental scales[21] may exaggerate the significance of clinical impressions that a child's intellectual endowment exceeds or falls short of the parents.'[31]

Our results show that battered children were in some respects lethargic. Difficult, especially crying or clinging, behaviour was encountered by the mothers and may have precipitated battering. After being some time in hos-pital, however, they were no more irritable than the controls. Thus, difficult behaviour probably results from interaction with a neurotic mother.[40] Our results bear this out.

Kempe[25] has asserted that in the prodromal stages mothers often and recurrently bring their infants with non-existent complaints and that family doctors are slow to identify and refer suspected cases.[46] We found, however, that no mother had made an unnecessary visit to her family doctor before the battering of her child. Indeed family doctors are unlikely to see more than one case in five years.[54] More characteristic was the long delay between injury and arrival at hospital, a factor also observed in other studies.[13,29]

Conclusion

In terms of morbidity and mortality the battered child is a problem of major concern to society. Child abuse has elicited spasmodic public concern for nearly a century, and yet no child protection service has developed that adequately meets the problem. It almost seems as if the medical profession has abdicated its responsibility to local authorities and voluntary organizations, whose roles in some respects are complementary but in others may not always be harmonious. Both agencies rely heavily upon inexperienced and possibly inadequately trained social workers who are as yet ill-equipped to deal with these difficult cases. The past year has again witnessed a depressing number of children who have been battered to death after decisions by social workers to return the child home. Our findings indicate that such authority should be curtailed. Indeed, there seems to be a strong case for setting up specialized hospital teams to carry out full assessment, giving priority to the safety and healthy development of the child.

We cannot predict which individual child will be battered. Nevertheless, our results[47,48,49] broadly delineate those groups in the community in which child abuse is most likely to occur. Prevention must rely on adequately designed, intensive education in children's needs and development during and after the antenatal stage. The high proportion of abnormalities at birth in our sample stresses the need to persuade these mothers to avail themselves of medical care. Without expert approaches to both these problems nearly all abused children are at risk of physical, educational, and social maldevelopment or death.

We thank Dr. K.W. Cross of the hospital statistics department who provided the figures for emergency and non-emergency admissions to Birmingham Children's Hospital and Mrs. Irene Brown and Mrs. Margaret Hall who helped with the statistical analysis. We are especially grateful to Professor W.H. Trethowan who provided valuable criticism and encouragement throughout the course of the study and to those paediatricians who referred patients to us. Dr. I.G.W. Pickering, Director of Prison Medical Services, allowed us to interview those patients in prison. Mrs. Sue Knight typed the manuscript. The study was supported by a grant from the Barrow and Geraldine Cadbury Trust.

References

1. Adelson, L. "Slaughter of the innocents: A study of forty-six homicides in which the victims were children." *New England Journal of Medicine* 264 (June, 1961):1345–1349.

2. "The battered baby." *British Medical Journal* 1 (March, 1966):601–603.

3. Butler, N.R. and Alberman, E.D. *The Second Report of the 1958 British Perinatal Mortality Survey.* Edinburgh: Livingstone, 1969.

4. Caffey, J. "Multiple fractures in the long bones of infants suffering from chronic subdural hematoma." *American Journal of Roentgenology* 56 (1946):163–173.

5. Cameron, J.M. "The battered baby syndrome." *The Practitioner* 209 (September, 1972):302–310.

6. City of Binghamton. *Abstract of Statistics 1970-71.* Central Statistics Office, City of Binghamton, 1972.

7. Cooper, C. Personal communication, 1974.

8. Crosse, V.M. *The Pre-Term Baby and other Babies with Low Weight.* Edinburgh: Livingstone: 1971.

9. Davids, A. and Holden, R.H. "Consistency of maternal attitudes and personality from pregnancy to eight months following childbirth." *Developmental Psychology* 2(3, 1970):364–366.

10. Drillien, C.M. *The Growth and Development of the Prematurely Born Infant.* Edinburgh: Livingstone, 1964.

11. Ebbin, A.J. et al. "Battered child syndrome at the Los Angeles County Hospital." *American Journal of Diseases in Children* 118 (October, 1969): 660–667.

12. Emery, J.L. "Welfare of families of children found unexpectedly dead ('cot death')." *British Medical Journal* 1 (March, 1972):612–615.

13. Gil, D.G. *Violence Against Children: Physical Child Abuse in the United States.* Cambridge: Harvard University Press, 1970.

14. Gregg, G.S. and Elmer, E. "Infant injuries: Accident or abuse?" *Paediatrics* 44 (September, 1969):434–439.

15. Griffiths, D.L. and Moynihan, F.J. "Multiple epiphysial injuries in babies ('Battered baby syndrome')." *British Medical Journal* 5372 (December, 1963):1558–1561.

16. Griffiths, R. *The Abilities of Babies.* London: University of London Press, 1954.

17. Guthkelch, A.N. "Infantile subdural haematoma and its relationship to whiplash injuries." *British Medical Journal* 2 (May, 1971):430–431.

18. Hall, M.H. Personal communication, 1974.

19. Harcourt, B. and Hopkins, D. "Ophthalmic manifestations of the battered baby syndrome." *British Medical Journal* 3 (August, 1971):398–401.

20. Helfer, R.E. "The responsibility and role of the physician," in *The Battered Child,* pp. 25–39. Edited by R.E. Helfer and C.H. Kempe. Chicago: University of Chicago Press, 1968.

21. Hindley, C.B. "Stability and change in abilities up to five years: Group trends." *Journal of Child Psychology and Psychiatry* 6(2, 1965):85–99.

22. Honzik, M.P. "Developmental studies of parent-child resemblances in intelligence." *Child Development* 28 (June, 1957):215–228.

23. *International Classification of Diseases.* Geneva: World Health Organization, 1968.

24. Kempe, C.H. et al. "The battered child syndrome." *JAMA* 181 (July, 1962):17–24.

25. Kempe, C.H. "Paediatric implications of the battered baby syndrome." *Archives of Diseases in Childhood* 46 (February, 1971):28–37.

26. Klaus, M.H. and Kennell, J.H. "Mothers separated from their newborn infants." *Pediatric Clinics of North America* 17 (November, 1970):1015–1037.

27. Klein, M. and Stern, L. "Low birth weight and the battered child syndrome." *American Journal of Diseases in Children* 122 (July, 1971):15–18.

28. Koel, B.S. "Failure to thrive and fatal injury as a continuum." *American Journal of Diseases in Children* 118 (October, 1969):565–567.

29. Lukianowicz, N. "Infanticide." *Psychiatric Clinica* 4(1971):145–158.

30. MacKeith, R. Personal communication, 1974.

31. Martin, H. "The child and his development," in *Helping the Battered Child and His Family*, pp. 93–114. Edited by R.E. Helfer and C.H. Kempe. Oxford: Lippincott, 1973.

32. Milowe, I.D. and Lourie, R.S. "The child's role in the battered child syndrome." *Journal of Pediatrics* 65 (November, 1964):1079–1081.

33. Mounsey, J. Personal communication, 1974.

34. Mushin, A.S. "Ocular damage in the battered baby syndrome." *British Medical Journal* 3 (August, 1971):402–404.

35. Newson, J. "Towards a theory of infant understanding." Unpublished, 1973.

36. Ounsted, C., Oppenheimer, R., and Lindsay, J. "Aspects of bonding failure: The psychopathology and psychotherapeutic treatment of families of battered children." *Developmental Medicine and Child Neurology* 16 (August, 1974):447–456.

37. Pohlman, E. *The Psychology of Birth Planning.* Cambridge: Schenkman Publishing Co., 1973.

38. Registrar General. *Statistical Review of England and Wales for 1971, Part 3.* London: H.M.S.O., 1973.

39. Richards, I.D. and McIntosh, H.T. "Confidential inquiry into 226 consecutive deaths." *Archives of Diseases in Childhood* 47 (October, 1972): 697–706.

40. Rutter, M. *Parents of Sick Children.* London: Oxford University Press, 1966.

41. Salmon, M.A. "The spectrum of abuse in the battered-child syndrome." *Injury* 2 (January, 1971):211–217.

42. Schaffer, H.R. Personal communication, 1974.

43. Schloesser, P.T. "The abused child." *Bulletin of the Menninger Clinic* 28 (September, 1964):260–268.

44. Silver, H.K. and Finkelstein, M. "Deprivation dwarfism." *Journal of Pediatrics* 70 (March, 1967):317–324.

45. Simons, B. et al. "Child abuse: Epidemiologic study of medically reported cases." *New York State Journal of Medicine* 66 (November, 1966): 2783–2788.

46. Skinner, A.E. and Castle, R.L. *Seventy-eight Battered Children: A Retrospective Study.* London: National Society for the Prevention of Cruelty to Children, 1969.

47. Smith, S.M. and Hanson, R. "Failure to thrive and anorexia nervosa." *Postgraduate Medical Journal* 48 (June, 1972):382–384.

48. Smith, S.M., Hanson, R., and Nobel, S. "Parents of battered babies: A controlled study." *British Medical Journal* 4 (November, 1973):388–391.

49. Smith, S.M., Hanson, R., and Noble, S. "Social aspects of battered baby syndrome." *British Journal of Psychiatry* 125 (December, 1974):568–582.

50. Steele, B.F. and Pollock, C.B. "A psychiatric study of parents who abuse infants and small children," in *The Battered Child,* pp. 89–133. Edited by R.E. Helfer and C.H. Kempe. Chicago: University of Chicago Press, 1968.

51. Stone, N.H. et al. "Child abuse by burning." *Surgical Clinics of North America* 50 (December, 1970):1419–1424.

52. Talukder, M.Q. and Dawson, K.P. "Nutritional marasmus in an affluent society." *The Practitioner* 212 (March, 1974):359–362.

53. Touloukian, R.J. "Abdominal visceral injuries in battered children." *Pediatrics* 42 (October, 1968):642–646.

54. *Turnbridge Wells Study Group on Non-Accidental Injury to Children.* London: Medical Education and Information Unit of the Spastics Society, 1973.

55. Vesterdal, J. *Annales Nestle* 27(1972):5.

56. "Violent parents." *Lancet* 2 (November, 1971):1017–1018.

57. Wadsworth, M. Personal communication, 1973.

58. Weston, J.T. "The pathology of child abuse," in *The Battered Child,* pp. 61–86. Edited by R.E. Helfer and C.H. Kempe. Chicago: University of Chicago Press, 1968.

59. Whitten, C.F., Pettit, M.G., and Fischhoff, J. "Evidence that growth failure from maternal deprivation is secondary to under eating." *JAMA* 209 (September, 1969):1675–1682.

60. Winick, M. "Malnutrition and brain development." *Journal of Pediatrics* 74 (May, 1969):667–679.

61. Woolley, P.V. and Evans, W.A. "Significance of skeletal lesions in infants resembling those of traumatic origin." *Journal of the American Medical Association* 158 (June, 1955):539–543.

7 Predictive Factors for Child Abuse

R.K. Oates, A.A. Davis and
M.G. Ryan

Although child abuse is a common problem, only 10% of battering parents have a recognizable psychiatric illness.[11] Superficially these families may be no different from those in the general community. Many of the background factors that are known to be associated with child abuse, such as disruption of mother/infant bonding,[6,8] social isolation[10] and diffuse social problems[7] are also found in families who do not abuse their children. Recent studies have attempted to predict families with the potential for child abuse in the maternity hospital[2,3] and in later childhood[9] so that a picture is now emerging of the characteristic features of families where child abuse is more likely to occur. However all of the factors so far identified can occur in families where child abuse does not, so that the clinical assessment of a family where child abuse is suspected remains difficult. For this reason it is important to continue to try to establish in what areas abusing and non-abusing families differ.

In this paper, fifty-six (56) families where child abuse and neglect had been documented were compared with a control group where there had been no concern about child abuse and neglect.

Patients and Methods

Out of a total of 187 cases of child abuse and neglect treated at the Royal Alexandra Hospital for Children, 56 children and their families were reviewed 1 to 3 years after their initial presentation. The 131 cases not reviewed were living too far from the hospital or unable to be traced. Each mother participated in a structured interview which enquired into the obstetric history, experiences with the child during the neonatal period, the parents' child-rearing practices and their expectations for the child. Problems of family health, housing, finance and domestic friction were explored and each child's development estimated using the Denver Developmental Screening Test. Each family was compared with a control family matched for education, employment, socio-economic status, nationality, marital status of the parents, and age, sex and health of the child. All families in the study group were registered with

Reprinted with permission from the *Australian Paediatric Journal* 16(4):239–243, R.K. Oates, A.A. Davis, and M.G. Ryan, "Predictive factors for child abuse," 1980.

Baby Health Centres, and control families were selected from the register of the Baby Health Centre in the same suburb. Two controls were chosen for each study family, one of which was selected at random and the other discarded. No regard was paid to regularity of attendance at the Baby Health Centre when controls were selected.

The mothers from the control group participated in the same structured interview as the study group mothers and the control children received the same developmental assessment.

Mothers in the control group were not aware that they were being compared with abusive families but agreed to be interviewed as part of a survey looking at child-rearing practices. All interviews in both groups were done by the one person (A.A.D.).

The results were compared by computer (Vogelback Computing Center, Northwestern University, Version 7.0, June 27, 1977) using the chi-squared test of significant differences.

Results

Mothers in the two groups perceived their childhood quite differently; 79% of the mothers from the child abuse and neglect group described their own childhood as lacking in affecting from their parents, compared with only 2% of controls.(P<.001). Thirty-seven percent of these mothers described their own mother's attitudes as being one of rejection compared with 2% of controls.

There was no significant difference between the ages of the mothers in the two groups when the index child was born. Fathers from the abuse and neglect group were younger than the control fathers; 25% of fathers from the abuse and neglect group were between 16 and 21 years of age when the child was born compared with 4% of fathers in the control group (P<.015).

There were significant differences in the pregnancies of the two groups. While 52% of pregnancies were unplanned in the abuse group, 27% were unplanned in the control group (P<.001).

Table 7-1
Name Chosen for Baby during Pregnancy

Name chosen	Only male names chosen	Only female names chosen	Name for either sex chosen
Abuse and neglect (56)	43%	23%	34%
Controls (56)	27%	16%	57%

$X^2 = 6.118$

$P = .05$

Table 7-2
Response of Fathers to News of Pregnancy

Reaction to pregnancy	Delighted	Generally pleased	Generally displeased	Father not aware of pregnancy
Abuse and neglect (56)	19%	43%	36%	2%
Controls (56)	63%	25%	12%	0%

The mothers in the abuse and neglect group were less likely to have made preparations, such as purchase of nappies and clothing for the baby's arrival; 46% of the study group had made preparation compared with 81% of controls (P<.002). The control family was more likely to have chosen a name for a boy and a girl during the pregnancy whereas the abuse and neglect family seemed to have expectations for the child even before birth, by more often choosing a name for only one sex as shown in table 7-1.

The father's reaction to the news of the pregnancy, as described by the mother, was less favourable in the abuse group (table 7-2); 36% of these fathers were reported to be displeased about the pregnancy compared with 12% of control fathers.

The births of the babies in the abuse group were reported as being more difficult and less pleasant. Obstetric complications, including prolonged labour, forceps delivery, unusual presentations, caesarean section or a combination of these factors occurred in 55% of the abuse group compared with 37% of controls (P<.001). The birth was described as a difficult or bad experience by 64% of mothers in the abuse group compared with 27% of controls (P<.001).

Prematurity or post-maturity occurred in 54% of the babies from the study group and in 13% of controls (P<.001). Medical problems in the first week of life, ranging from respiratory distress syndrome, apnaea and infection

Table 7-3
Mothers' Perception of Child as a Baby

Description of baby	Ideal	Above average	Reasonable	Below average	Very poor
Abuse and neglect (56)	18%	25%	12%	25%	20%
Controls (56)	25%	45%	27%	3%	0%

$X^2 = 7.11$

$P = .008$

Table 7–4
Commencement of Toilet Training

Age toilet-training commenced	Under 6-months	6-11 months	12-17 months	18-23 months	24 months and over
Abuse and neglect (56)	25%	23%	20%	11%	21%
Controls (56)	0%	5%	20%	46%	29%

$X^2 = 33.32$
$P < .0001$

through to mild jaundice and feeding problems occurred in 52% of babies from the abuse group and in 9% of controls ($P < .001$). These factors may have contributed to the lower incidence of attempted breast-feeding in the study group which was 20% compared with 66% of controls ($P < .001$).

To find out what sort of experiences the mothers had with their children in the first few months of life, they were asked to rate their memories of the child as a baby on a scale ranging from ideal to very poor. Table 7–3 shows that while the control mothers tended to think that their babies had been at least reasonable, and often above average, many of the mothers in the abuse and neglect group saw their babies as being below average. When asked if they enjoyed caring for their child, 34% of mothers from the abuse group stated that they did not. This response was not made by any mothers from the control group.

The expectations the two groups of parents had for their children, were compared by asking about toilet-training and behaviour. Table 7–4 shows that the parents from the abuse and neglect group commenced toilet-training much earlier, often before 12 months of age, that the control parents, who were more likely to commence toilet-training after 18 months. In addition to

Table 7–5
Strictness of Toilet Training

Method of training	Left on pot for long periods, accidents punished	Put on pot regularly, moderate disapproval for accidents	Trained when child seems ready, no scolding
Abuse and neglect (56)	30%	50%	20%
Controls (56)	0%	50%	50%

$X^2 = 24.41$
$P < .0001$

Table 7-6
Praise for Good Behavior

Praise given	Rarely	Sometimes	Readily
Abuse and neglect (56)	45%	37%	18%
Controls (56)	0%	27%	73%

$X^2 = 44.84$
$P < .001$

the high expectations for toilet-training, punishment in trying to achieve bowel control was used much more frequently than in the control group. Table 7-5 shows that the control parents were more tolerant and far less punitive than the abuse families who often made the child sit on the pot for long periods and meted out punishment for soiling.

There were significant differences between the two groups in the use of physical punishment for discipline. Fifty-four percent of mothers in the abuse and neglect group said that they used physical punishment frequently compared with 11% of control ($P < .001$). When verbal punishment was used, the children from the abuse group were told that they were bad or not loved in 41% of cases, compared with this approach in 2% of controls ($P < .001$). Control mothers were more likely to deal with temper tantrums by going to another room and leaving the child (55% compared with 29% from the abuse group) whereas the study mothers were more likely to react to temper tantrums by screaming back at the child or hitting him (55% compared with 12% of controls ($P < .001$).

When children from the abuse group were good, they were rarely praised for it. Table 7-6 shows that the children from the control group were likely to be praised readily by their parents when they were good compared with children in the abuse group who were rarely praised for good behaviour.

Table 7-7
Supervision Provided by Mothers

Supervision	Checks frequently	Checks fairly often	Practically never checks
Abuse and neglect (56)	21%	38%	41%
Controls (56)	62%	36%	2%

$X^2 = 31.44$
$P < .001$

Table 7–8
Fathers' Interest in Child

Fathers' interest in child	Very fond of child	Quite fond of child	Rejects child or not interested
Abuse and neglect (56)	14%	38%	48%
Controls (56)	69%	20%	11%

$X^2 = 37.07$
$P < .001$

Parents in the abuse and neglect group were stricter than the control parents with regard to jumping on furniture, and making a mess (86% compared with 68% of controls); however, they were less likely to know what their children were doing at a particular moment and checked on their whereabouts and activities less frequently than the control mothers. Table 7–7 shows that the control mothers provided a higher level of supervision.

The mothers in the study group thought highly of their partners in 7% of cases and 54% of them thought poorly of their partner. This compares with the control group where 43% thought highly of their partners and 11% held their partners in poor regard ($P<.001$).

Important decisions in the abuse and neglect families were shared between the partners in 27% of cases. Fifty-four percent of control parents shared important decisions ($P<.02$). Frequent disagreement between the study partners about child rearing matters occurred in 30% of cases and 46% did not discuss child-rearing practices together at all. This compares with 2% disagreement in the controls and non-participation in 36% ($P<.001$).

When the mothers were asked how the child's father got on with the child, 48% of fathers in the abuse and neglect group were said to be not interested in the child. Table 7–8 shows the differences in the mothers' perception of how the fathers in the two groups related to the child.

The mothers from the abuse and neglect group had social contact with people less frequently than the controls. Table 7–9 shows that while 59% of

Table 7–9
Social Life of Mother

Contact with other people	Almost daily	Weekly	Infrequently	Very rarely
Abuse and neglect (56)	34%	16%	29%	21%
Controls (56)	59%	32%	7%	2%

$X^2 = 22.73$
$P < .001$

Table 7-10
Areas of Family Stress

Problem	Finance	Housing	Domestic friction	Own health	Health of family
Abuse and neglect (56)	64%	38%	50%	46%	54%
Controls (56)	32%	9%	5%	4%	14%
	$X^2=10.34$	$X^2=11.27$	$X^2=25.69$	$X^2=25.19$	$X^2=17.56$
	$P < .002$	$P < .001$	$P < .001$	$P < .001$	$P < .001$

controls had daily social contact, this was so for only one third of the study group and many of the mothers had very little social contact at all. Opportunities to get away from their child for short periods were less common in the study group; 48% used babysitters compared with 85% of controls ($P<.001$).

The abuse and neglect families were larger than the control families; 29% of these families had four or more children compared with 14% of controls ($P<.003$).

There were no differences in the nominated religious affiliation of the two groups but those in the control group attended church more frequently. In the study group 75% of mothers never attended church compared with 38% of controls while 41% of controls attended church at least monthly compared with 20% of study mothers ($P<.001$).

Differences between the two groups were found in finance, housing, domestic friction and health in the family. Table 7-10 shows that in the abuse and neglect group financial problems were twice as common, problems in inadequate housing were four times commoner and serious domestic friction was ten times commoner. Poor health occurred eleven times more often in the mothers and other members of the family were four times more likely to have health problems than control families.

An estimate of the development level of each of the two groups of children, using the Denver Developmental Screening Test, showed that children from the child abuse and neglect group were more likely to have two or more delays in the various sub-tests. This was particularly marked in the language sub-test with 36% showing two or more delays compared with 8% of controls.

Discussion

These two groups of families are superficially similar in terms of marital status. However, there are marked differences in the areas of the mother's childhood and her experiences during the pregnancy and perinatal period, the expectations for the child, child-rearing techniques, family and community support, health of the parents and development of the child.

Table 7-11

Percentage Showing Two or More Delays in Each Sub-Test of the Denver Development Screening Test

Test item	Personal-social	Fine motor-adaptive	Language	Gross motor
Abuse and neglect	11%	14%	36%	18%
Controls	5%	2%	8%	2%
Significance	$X^2=7.99\%$	$X^2=11.78$	$X^2=18.58$	$X^2=14.29$
	$P < .05$	$P < .01$	$P < .001$	$P < .003$

In a study such as this it is difficult to be sure about the validity of the retrospective information obtained from the mothers about their pregnancy, the child's birth, the neonatal period and the child's early development. Whether the material they recalled was quite accurate or not is less important than the fact that these mothers, when compared with the controls perceived the birth as being difficult, the father being unsupportive and the child difficult. From the results of this study, a profile emerges of the family where child abuse is more likely to occur.

The pregnancy is often unplanned and father, who may be young, is likely to be unhappy about the pregnancy. The mother, who has often experienced insufficient mothering in her own childhood, may do very little to prepare for the child's arrival and her expectations for the child may be established before birth when she chooses a name for only one sex. The birth is often a complicated one and is seen by the mother as being an unpleasant experience. The child is likely to have a medically complicated neonatal period which may interfere with the establishment of the mother/infant bond.

As the baby grows into infancy, he is seen by the parents as comparing unfavourably with other children. Childrearing techniques are likely to be strict although there is little positive encouragement or supervision of the child. This puts the child in the difficult position of being supervised infrequently by parents who have high expectations and who are more likely to punish the child when he gets into trouble, even though this behaviour may result from lack of supervision. The high expectations are exemplified by the approach to toilet-training which is commenced early and is likely to be punitive.

Decisions about child management are not discussed between the parents and child-rearing responsibilities are often not shared at all. The spouse is likely to be held in low regard by the other partner. Contact with other adults outside the family is infrequent and there are few opportunities to be relieved from the burden of constantly caring for a child who is seen as unrewarding.

Domestic friction is common and this is complicated by accommodation difficulties, and unsatisfactory budgeting of family finances. Problems of poor health in the parents and other family members are particularly common. A comparison of these two groups of children on a simple developmental screening scale suggests that the development of abused children, when compared with controls, may be delayed. Further detailed follow-up studies of abused children are required to clarify this.

The increased risk of child abuse when the pregnancy is complicated by premature delivery and neonatal problems, is well recognised.[1,5] This study confirms these findings and also highlights the increased incidence of complicated deliveries, which might have contributed to so many of the mothers in this study describing the birth as a bad experience. Maternal ill-health has only recently been described[6] as contributing to child abuse in families which have other risk factors. This study shows that health problems are much commoner in all family members when compared with controls.

Studies have shown that families with the potential to abuse their children may be able to be detected in the maternity hospital[7] and in ante-natal clinics.[4] The factors in this study which distinguish the abuse and neglect families from the controls are not difficult to detect and should be looked for in ante-natal clinics, maternity hospitals, and by nursing and medical staff who come into contact with young children and their families.

As child abuse is likely to occur in successive generations, it is important that medical and nursing personnel who deal with parents and children, should be aware of the risk factors associated with child abuse, so that appropriate steps can be taken to intervene to break this cycle. Some of the risk factors which are commonly found in abusing and neglectful families, when compared with controls, have been shown in this study. This is not to suggest that all mothers identified by these factors are liable to child abuse. However it is possible that many of the abusing families within the community will be located within the larger group identified by these factors. As additional health and social work resources are limited, it is suggested that they be directed towards the group which could be identified by the factors shown in this study.

References

1. Baldwin, J.A. and Oliver, J.E. "Epidemiology and family characteristics of severely abused children." *British Journal of Preventive Social Medicine* 29 (December, 1975):205–221.

2. Frommer, E.A., and O'Shea, G. "Antenatal identification of women liable to have problems in managing their infants." *British Journal of Psychiatry* 123 (August, 1973):149–156.

3. Geddis, D.C., Monaghan, S.M., Muir, R.C. and Jones, C.J. "Early prediction in the maternity hospital—The Queen Mary Child Care Unit." *Child Abuse and Neglect* 3(3–4, 1979):757–766.

4. Gray, J.D., Cutler, C.A., Dean, J.G. and Kempe, C.H. "Prediction and prevention of child abuse and neglect." *Child Abuse and Neglect* 1(1, 1977):45–58.

5. Klein, M. and Stern, L. "Low birth weight and the battered child syndrome." *American Journal of Diseases of Children* 122 (July, 1971):15–18.

6. Lynch, M.A. "Ill health and child abuse." *Lancet* 2 (August, 1975): 317–319.

7. Lynch, M.A., Roberts, R., and Gordon, M. "Child abuse: Early warning in the maternity hospital." *Developmental Medicine and Child Neurology* 18(6, 1976):759.

8. Ounsted, C., Oppenheimer, R., and Lindsay, J. "Aspects of bonding failure: The psychopathology and psychotherapeutic treatment of families of battered children." *Developmental Medicine and Child Neurology* 16 (August, 1974):447–456.

9. Robertson, B.A. and Juritz, J.M. "Characteristics of families of abused children." *Child Abuse and Neglect* 3(3–4, 1979):857–862.

10. Ryan, M.G., Davis, A.A., and Oates, R.K. "One hundred and eighty-seven cases of child abuse and neglect." *Medical Journal of Australia* 2 (November, 1977):623–628.

11. Steele, B.F. and Pollock, C.B. "A psychiatric study of parents who abuse small children," in *The Battered Child,* pp. 89–133. Edited by R.E. Helfer and C.H. Kempe. Chicago: The University of Chicago Press, 1968.

8

Child Abuse in India and the Nutritionally Battered Child

A.K. Bhattacharyya

Introduction

Cruelty to children has been for ages a part of human behaviour all over the globe[29] and India is no exception. Accounts of infanticide are available in Hindu mythology and there are anecdotes on children being sacrificed for achieving divine favour in ancient times. It was only in the earlier part of the nineteenth century that the prejudicial practice of throwing children into the holy river Ganges at its mouth where it enters the Bay of Bengal was abolished by law. Female infanticide was practiced by the Rajputs, faced with the difficulty of getting their daughters married.[28] Infanticide perhaps existed elsewhere in the country for various other reasons. Corporal punishment was very common in schools about three decades back.

These forms of cruelties to children differ considerably from willful but unadmitted and often repetitive physical abuse which is characteristic of the classical 'battered child syndrome'[23] now called 'non-accidental injury' in the United Kingdom and 'the abused child' in the United States. With growing concern for healthy child growth and development however, the problem of child abuse should be considered in a much wider sense. While physical assault is commonly reported from the affluent countries, children are subjected to various other forms of inhuman treatment in the socio-cultural and economic milieu of the third world.

With the object of showing the nature and extent of the problem of child abuse in India, this paper (i) reviews briefly the few published Indian reports of classical battered baby cases, (ii) puts forward a wider concept of child abuse and describes the prevailing forms including nutritional deprivation and (iii) characterizes two hitherto unrecognized syndromes of prolonged and severe protein-energy malnutrition (PEM) suggesting the term 'nutritionally battered child' for the victim of either syndrome.

Adapted with permission from *Child Abuse and Neglect* 3(2), A.K. Bhattacharyya, "Child abuse in India and nutritionally battered child," 1979. Pergamon Press, Ltd.

Classical Battered Baby Cases in India

The First Report

A 22-month-old girl and her 10-month-old brother, from a middle income family, were admitted to the hospital attached to the Calcutta School of Tropical Medicine, in April 1966 for having recurrent painful swelling of limbs during the previous 3 months. Radiological pictures were suggestive of multiple fractures of long bones, epiphyseal separations and periosteal reactions. Subsequently, it was revealed that a caretaker subjected the sibs to repeated physical assaults out of jealousy. The sibs could be protected against further abuse. When these two cases were presented in a Clinical Meeting[3], the condition seemed to be unknown to the audience. Hence, they were reported subsequently in detail with a review of the literature.[4]

Subsequent Studies

The author has come across only four papers[4,25,26,33] on battered child syndrome in India giving accounts of altogether 12 cases. One case recently seen by the author remains unpublished. Of these 13 cases, 3 were from Calcutta, 2 from Bombay, 3 from Madras and 5 from Poona. Two were newborns and the ages of others were between 1 and 6 months in 3, 6 and 12 months in 2, 18 and 24 months in 4, and 24 and 30 months in 2; 6 were males and 5 females and the sex was not reported in 2. The socio-economic condition of the 12 families was high in 2, medium in 2, low in 2, very low in 1 and not stated in 5. The nature of the injuries were: bony fractures with or without epiphyseal separations and periosteal reactions in 7 (involving multiple long bones in 5, multiple long bones and skull bones with ecchymoses and burn scars in 1 and only one humerus in 1), compression fractures of ribs in 1 (newborn), only periosteal reactions in 1 and repeated epistaxis and bruises in 3. One was brought to hospital as having died suddenly. A jealous caretaker was the batterer in 2 sibs, a hostile female cousin in 1, the mother in 7 and the father in 1. In 2, the batterer could not be identified but in 1 case the father was probably responsible. The battering was caused by the mother in one case as the baby had harelip and cleft palate, she being the sixth successive child born with such defects. Unhappy relations with the husband due to presence of a co-wife was responsible in another. In the third case, the mother was deserted by her husband following the birth of the baby and she felt that the child was responsible for all the misfortune that had befallen her. Three other mothers injured their children (epistaxis and bruises) as "he/she is too bad and gets on to my nerves." [25] Yet another had already 6 children and was not keen to have another. The battering father of one 18-month-old child, brought dead to the hospital, without any external injury (autopsy not permitted), developed one year later a psychiatric illness resulting from a guilt complex and confessed of having beaten the child for a minor fault, never thinking of fatal consequences.[25] Except in this case and in another, the assaults were repetitive in all others and 3 (out of 13) died. Failure to thrive was recorded in only 2.

Comments

The causes of child abuse in the Indian cases reviewed here, do not differ essentially from those reported from the developed countries. In India, remarkable socio-economic changes have taken place during the last three decades. There is increasing urbanization but facilities for housing, transport, good schools and recreation are often very inadequate. Also the age-old large joint families are being replaced by nuclear families and the number of working mothers are increasing. They have fewer children (mostly one or two) now but there is often no creche for the babies and usually they are looked after by maids. In the economically weaker section of the community, poverty may contribute significantly towards child abuse. The environmental factors are therefore unfavourable and there must be many parents psychologically prone to be batterers.[15] It is very likely that physical assault does occur and many cases go unreported. But despite these, it also appears that the magnitude must be much less in comparison to that in the developed countries. However, socio-anthropological studies must be very extensive to throw any light on the possible magnitude and nature of child battering in a country like India.

Child Abuse in a Wider Sense

The Concept

Human development. A WHO Scientific Group[37] has considered that human development embraces every aspect of the maturation process taking place in the human life cycle. It is characterized by phases and transitional events. The development of the child begins in the mother's womb with the fertilization of the ovum and continues in the subsequent phases—the foetal life, the breast dependence and weaning ages and the pre-school and school years. It is influenced by genetic factors and directly or indirectly, by environmental factors—physical, chemical, biological and social—of which economic condition of the family, education and cultural beliefs and changes in human setting (urbanization for example) are very important ones. Healthy development depends upon the utilization of many areas of scientific knowledge and many components of the health service such as nutrition, communicable diseases, human reproduction and many others. There are critical periods of growth and development[31] and clinical and experimental observations show that nutritional failure at younger ages can have permanent consequences.

Child abuse.   In accordance with the concept of human development quoted above, one can justifiably suggest that child abuse should be defined in a wider sense, as impaired development of a child for a considerable period or death resulting from any adverse environmental factor that could otherwise be prevented to operate on the basis of scientific knowledge and adequate health services. Further, if this insult is of such a nature in duration and degree that it causes physical disability or mental impairment or both persisting throughout life, this must be considered a very serious form of child abuse. The factors responsible for such child abuse are broadly those involved in healthy child development. The critical period is up to the pre-school age.

The Background

Country size and population.   India is a vast subcontinent with an area of about 32.8 million square kilometers and according to 1971 census,[21] a population of 548 million. About 80% lives in nearly 0.6 million villages with poor transport and communication systems and 20% in about 3000 cities and towns. Children under 14 constitute 41.6% and children under 6, 17% (115 million) of the population. Child mortality (described later) is high but this is overcompensated by high birth rate (35.2% in 1975) and a fall in crude death rate (14.7%) resulting from increase in the average life expectancy (46.4 for males and 45.6 for females) during the last 30 years.

Poverty.   A substantial proportion of the population lives below the poverty line or the subsistence level. At 1960-61 prices, this has been considered to be at the level of per capita annual income of 340 Indian rupees or about 43 dollars. In terms of 1973-74 consumers' expenditure, those having a monthly income of 61.80 rupees in rural areas and those having a monthly income of 71.30 rupees in cities are taken to be below the poverty line. According to various sources 40% to 60% of the people live under the poverty line and 25% are very poor. About 40% of the 115 million children live under the poverty line.[21]

Unemployment.   At present, there are about 10 million educated and enlisted unemployed persons. A substantial proportion, particularly from the rural areas is not enlisted and there is a huge illiterate and unemployed or underemployed mass.

Illiteracy.   In 1971, the literacy rate, excluding the children under-five, was 21.48% for females and 45.28% for males and 33.84% for the females and males combined. The literacy rate for the urban population was 59.7% compared to only 27.0% for the rural population. Eighty-six percent of children enter school; those who do not are mostly girls or children from weaker sections of the community. However, of those enrolled in schools, only 40% reach grade V and only 25% reach grade VIII.[21]

Housing problem.   In most cities, accommodation is inadequate and too costly. Many live in congested and filthy slums. In Calcutta, it has been estimated that about 35,000 dwell in pavements where babies are also born and reared.

Child feeding.   There is a declining trend in breast feeding, depriving the child from the natural, and hygienic food of great economic value.[2] Otherwise, breast feeding is a usual practice, particularly in rural areas. It is often prolonged but hardly adequate after 6 months. However, the proportion of capable mothers varies in different parts of the country.[1,9,12,14,21] Supplements usually consist of diluted and/or insufficient cow milk or powder and gruels prepared of barley, sago, rice, etc. Solids are started after 6 months or even later and complete weaning to cereal-based diets is achieved by 18 months of age in the majority (but not in all) under 'favourable' circumstances. Obviously, this diet is nutritionally inadequate in energy, protein and most other nutrients.

Socio-cultural aspects.   The socio-cultural complexities and diversities of the vast Indian subcontinent are intriguing. A huge poor and illiterate or poorly educated mass living in its rural and tribal areas follows largely a traditional life (with old customs and beliefs and methods of child feeding and rearing) which however, is continuously being subjected to modifications under the influence of several rapidly developing industrial zones. The 1971 census recorded that 19.87% of the population was urban. In 1961 census, this figure was 17.98%. However, as the population has increased, actually much more people now live in urban areas. For various reasons, the impact of family planning programs has fallen mostly on higher income group. Low income families, both in urban and in rural areas, are often larger families (5 or 6 children) with larger number of children of lesser ages; infections and severe nutritional deficiencies are also more frequent in such families.[9,12] Morbidity depends more on family income rather than on its unitary or joint character.[21]

Medical education and health services.   The western-model of medical education followed in the Medical colleges is not considered suitable for the country's need.[5,13,21,27,32] The young specialty of paediatrics is developing fast but mostly in teaching institutions. As stated elsewhere, "paediatric nutrition receives almost fragmentary consideration in our undergraduate teaching."[5] Health services available mostly in cities and towns are not adequate particularly for the low-income group. However, the real problem is rural health care. The Primary Health Centre, each for a population of about

80,000 to 120,000 and with sub-centres, at an average of one for every 10,000 population, functions to provide medical services in all possible forms to in-patients, out-patients and the community. Insufficient medical and para-medical manpower and administrative factors are important reasons for the unsatisfactory working of this vast infra-structure.[32]

Forms of Child Abuse

Mortality and morbidity. Perinatal mortality rate (1969 figure) is 63.8 and still birth rate 22.1. Infant mortality rate (1971 figure) is 122 (81 in urban areas and 131 in rural areas).[21] Of the total mortality, 37.5% is contributed by mortality in children under 5 years of age.[34] Only 72% of all those born alive complete 5 years of age. Of the perinatal deaths, 60 to 70% are associated with low birth weight, notably due to maternal malnutrition[12] which is directly related to socio-economic status.[16] By far the most important causes of high childhood morbidity are communicable and preventable infections and mal-nutrition and very often one favours the other worsening the situation. The morbidity pattern is fairly uniform for rural or urban areas.[21] Available data based on hospital statistics show that intestinal infections constitute 7 to 15% of all admissions of under-fives. Also of the total admissions in all age groups, 30 to 40% are for all intestinal infections and 55 to 70% for all cases of enteritis and other diarrhoeal diseases in under-fives.[21] The concept of weanling diarrhoea[20] is helpful to understand the effect of inadequate weaning food contaminated with infections. Bacterial invasion of small bowel is a signifi-cant cause of diarrhoea in malnourished children.[9,27] The incidence of common intestinal parasitic infections (ascaris, giardia, hookworm and amoeba) in different parts of the country varies from 13.2 to 78%.[21,24] Res-piratory tract infections (bacterial and viral), boils, measles, diphtheria, whooping cough, and tetanus (notably neonatal) are significant contributors to mortality and morbidity.[9,21] Available epidemiological data indicate the prevalence of tuberculosis in children below the age of 14 years as 2.7%. The annual incidence of new cases is 1.09% and 40% of child population below 14 years and 25% of those below 6 years are positive tuberculin reactors.[18] Pulmonary, meningeal, visceral and miliary forms are common in hospital practice and 30% of those with meningeal lesions die.[35] About 20% of severe-ly malnourished children have pulmonary lesions radiologically, this being very advanced in 8%.[9]

Malnutrition. By far the commonest form of nutritional failure in chil-dren is protein-energy malnutrition (PEM).[9] A survey has shown that amongst the under-fives, clinically 2% suffer from severe forms of PEM and 20% from mild-moderate forms.[22] The prevalence of mild-moderate cases will be much higher (60 to 80%) if anthropometric criteria are used.[19] In view of the high mortality and morbidity[9,34] and significant dwarfism and delayed mental development[8] PEM must be regarded as a serious form of child abuse and neglect. Two other nutritional deficiencies, xerophthalmia and rickets, produce permanent and serious disabilities. Xerophthalmia is seen in 2 to 5% of pre-school children.[12,22] About 20%[9] of those with severe PEM develop keratomalacia, a most important cause of preventable blindness. Nutritional rickets occurs with varying regional prevalence, this being 1.8%[12] in Calcutta. At times it takes very severe atrophic forms.[10]

Some classical battered baby cases may fail to thrive. This is well known. Conversely however, as a malnourished child lacks in charm and demands more parental care, thereby decreasing their earning capacity, he may be deprived of affection. It is not known whether this leads to any physical assault or intentional neglect contributing towards recurrent malnutrition commonly observed.[8]

Exploitation. Born in poverty and squalor, brought up under deprivation of minimum prerequisites for healthy development, the lives of a large proportion of children are obviously miserable and they have no future. On the contrary, many of these poor human offspring are exploited in various ways. Under economic compulsions, low income families use their manual labour in agriculture and in urban areas. They are employed in small trades, in houses, hotels and restaurants (mostly boys) or in hazardous jobs at a very tender age. The worst form of exploitation is however beggary, which ruins the very social and psychological make-up of the growing mind. Beggary is common in children of pavement dwellers in Calcutta and in some other areas (but not in all cities). It is also seen in temples, railway stations and trains. Some are blind or possess grotesque physical deformities. The fact that they are seen to survive for several years in pitiable health, in the same locality raises strong suspicion that the crippling has been done deliberately by their 'caretakers.' Yet another sin is to trap somehow very young girls to utilize them later as prostitutes. Some reports appear at times in news papers on these types of child abuse but the magnitude has never been assessed and it is impossible to substantite these reports.

Nutritionally Battered Children

Common Types of PEM

The clinical types of severe PEM, commonly seen in Calcutta[9] are: the fatty type including 'classical kwashiorkor' and 'kwashiorkor without dermatosis' and the wasted type including 'nutritional marasmus' and 'marasmic kwashiorkor'. Anthropometrically, both the types show growth failure. Compared to Harvard standard, usually, in the fatty type the weight for age is between

50 and 60%, the height for age between 75 and 85% and the weight for height between 70 and 90% and in the wasted type these are between 35 and 45%, 65 and 85% and 50 and 70% respectively. A common milder form is 'pre-kwashiorkor' which shows no oedema, wasting or skin change but the weight for age, the height for age and the weight for height are usually as low as in the fatty type.[6,9] The WHO classification on PEM[36] is inadequate for many children and particularly for those with pre-kwashiorkor. In a survey, 11% of under-fives were below 60% of weight for age but only 1.83% were clinically marasmic.[14]

The Nutritionally Battered Child

It is generally accepted that a child with kwashiorkor may subsequently develop marasmus if treatment is inadequate and a marasmic child may come later with marasmic kwashiorkor. Less commonly, after a period of recovery, a marasmic child may develop 'fatty' kwashiorkor. Majority of children with severe or mild-moderate PEM survive, get accustomed to a cereal-based family diet, and reach population normal and a smaller proportion dies.[8] However, occasionally weaning is grossly unsatisfactory, intercurrent infections recur too frequently and it may so happen that (i) the pre-kwashiorkor state lingers for years, no history (admittedly, may not be reliable in all) of oedema or emaciation is available and the child remains incredibly small or (2) the child suffers recurrently from kwashiorkor or marasmus with short periods of incomplete recovery from either condition but somehow escapes death. In these two situations, the resulting pictures are extremely severe types of PEM, not described in the available literature. The first type has been called[7] 'prolonged pre-kwashiorkor' (PPK) and the second[11] 'recurrent kwashiorkor-marasmus' (RKM). A detailed study of these syndromes will be published elsewhere but their chief characteristics are described here. While PEM should be regarded as a serious form of child abuse, the term, "Nutritionally Battered Child" is suggested particularly for a child with PPK or RKM as both the syndromes result from prolonged and/or repetitive assaults of very severe malnutrition. The prevalence of these syndromes in the community is not known but PPK and RKM were diagnosed in 40 (.073%) out of 5460 children attending the under-seven Tropical Paediatric Clinic during 1973–1977. During 1967–77, 37 such children, aged 2 to 7 years, could be hospitalized and followed up. The characteristics common to PPK and RKM are: (1) age 2 to 7 years, (2) gross dietary deficiency of energy, protein and other nutrients from early infancy, (3) recurrent diarrhoea and/or respiratory infections, (4) extreme retardation in growth (compared to Harvard standard, weight for age 25 to 40%, height for age 60 to 70% and weight for height 55 to 75%) and development (inability even to stand and to talk), (5) significant hypoalbuminaemia,

(6) moderate anaemia, (7) no apparent cause of failure in growth and development except malnutrition and associated infections and (8) clinical and biochemical improvement with adequate diet given for 3 to 6 months in the hospital when they gain in weight, learn to stand, walk and talk but develop a state of dwarfing with still grossly low weight for age and height for age and normal weight for height. The distinguishing features between RKM and PPK are wasting and oedema which are recurrent in RKM but surprisingly not seen in PPK. The long-term effects on physical and mental developments remain to be studied.

Protection

It will be grossly incorrect to assume from the foregoing discussions that nothing has so far been done to protect the huge child population at risk against abuse in the wider sense. The Constitution of the Republic of India has specified the needs of the children and the duty of the community in meeting them adequately. In fact, there have been many attempts[17,21,30] to improve the situation. Measures adopted by the Indian Council of Child Welfare and the Department of Social Welfare under the five-year plans, through the network of social welfare institutions and community programs, indicate special concern for the physical, emotional and social care of children. Also there are provisions in the special laws relating to children for their welfare, development and protection. Many States have passed anti-beggary legislation. In others, Municipal and Police Acts provide for measures against begging. Provisions have also been made for rehabilitation and healthy development of children found begging. Factories Act, 1962, statutorily lays down for establishment of creches in every factory where the number of women employees exceeds 50. Employment of young children in factories, shops and establishments is also governed by law. There is definitely increasingly more move to improve health care for rural people—school health and child health services —health and nutrition education and education of children. Reorientation of paediatric medical education has also been under consideration keeping in mind the national needs. More and more emphasis has been laid on the implementation of family planning programs. The Integrated Child Development Services (ICDS) scheme which is now being implemented in a number of project areas is a step towards human resource development. ICDS provides a package of services; supplementary nutrition, immunization, health check-up referral services, health and nutrition education and non-formal pre-school education. With encouraging results, the project areas are being gradually extended. However, it would appear that the different measures that have been adopted so far are perhaps too many. Successful implementation of them depends on the co-ordination of several governmental departments and this may be difficult to achieve due to bureaucratic affairs. Failure to involve the community is another important deterrent.

Acknowledgement

Grateful thanks are due to Prof. A.B. Chowdhury, Director, School of Tropical Medicine, Calcutta, for his kind permission to publish this paper. It is regretted that of the works that have been consulted, many important ones, particularly the individual contributions to the book, "The child in India"[21] could not be quoted.

References

1. Belavady, B. "Nutrition in pregnancy and lactation." *Indian Journal of Medical Research* 57 (August, 1969):8.

2. Berg, A. *The Nutrition Factor.* Washington, D.C.: Brookings Institution, 1973.

3. Bhattacharyya, A.K. "Multiple fractures." *Bulletin of the Calcutta School of Tropical Medicine* 14 (July, 1966):111–112.

4. Bhattacharyya, A.K. and Mandal, J.N. "Battered child syndrome: A review with a report of two siblings." *Indian Pediatrics* 4 (April, 1967):186–194.

5. Bhattacharyya, A.K. "The need of pediatric nutrition units." *Calcutta Medical Journal* 68 (1971):233.

6. Bhattacharyya, A.K. "Pre-kwashiorkor." *Bulletin of the Calcutta School of Tropical Medicine* 21 (January, 1973):17–18.

7. Bhattacharyya, A.K. "Prolonged pre-kwashiorkor." *Bulletin of the Calcutta School of Tropical Medicine* 23 (1975):22.

8. Bhattacharyya, A.K. "Studies on kwashiorkor and marasmus in Calcutta (1957–74) III. Therapeutic and follow-up studies." *Indian Pediatrics* 12 (November, 1975):1125–1133.

9. Bhattacharyya, A.K. "Studies on kwashiorkor and marasmus in Calcutta. (1957–74), I. Aetiological and clinical studies." *Indian Pediatrics* 12 (November, 1975):1103–1113.

10. Bhattacharyya, A.K. and Dutta, K.N. "Atrophic rickets (with case reports)." *Indian Pediatrics* 30 (1976):267.

11. Bhattacharyya, A.K. "Recurrent kwashiorkor-marasmus." *Bulletin of the Calcutta School of Tropical Medicine* 26 (1978): in press.

12. Chaudhuri, M.K. "Nutrition profile of Calcutta pre-school children II. Clinical observations." *Indian Journal of Medical Research* 63 (February, 1975):173–188.

13. Chowdhury, A.B. "Tropical diseases in the tropics." *Journal of the Indian Medical Association* 69 (December, 1977):266–267.

14. Chowdhury, M. et al. "Breast feeding by urban mothers." *Journal of the Indian Medical Association* 70 (May, 1978):221–224.

15. Court, J. "Characteristics of parents and children," in *The Maltreated Child,* pp. 27–39. Edited by J. Carter. London: Priory Press, 1974.

16. Datta Banik, N.D. "A study on incidence of different birth weight babies and related factors." *Indian Pediatrics* 15 (April, 1978):327–334.

17. Devadas, R.P. and Murthy, N.K. "Nutrition of the pre-school child in India." *World Review of Nutrition and Dietetics* 27 (1977):1–33.

18. Dingley, H.B. "Tuberculosis in India." *Indian Pediatrics* 13 (December, 1976):879–880.

19. Gopalan, C. and Vijayaraghavan, K. *Nutrition Atlas of India.* Hyderbad: National Institute of Nutrition, 1971.

20. Gordon, J.E., Chitkara, I.D., and Wyon, J.B. "Weanling diarrhoea." *American Journal of the Medical Sciences* 245 (March, 1963):129–136.

21. Gupta, S. ed. *The Child In India.* New Delhi: Indian Pediatrics, 1977.

22. Indian Council of Medical Research. *Studies on Pre-School Chilren,* Technical Report series No. 26, New Delhi, 1974.

23. Kempe, C.H. et al. "The battered child syndrome." *JAMA* 181 (July, 1962):17–24.

24. Madan, S., Ghosal, S.P. and Sengupta, P.C. "Intestinal parasitosis: Its relation to diarrhoea in Indian children." *Indian Pediatrics* 14 (1977):899.

25. Magotra, M.L. "Battered baby syndrome." *Archives of Child Health* 18 (1976):41.

26. Merchant, S.M. et al. "The battered child syndrome." *Pediatric Clinics of India* 2 (1967):170.

27. Morley, D. *Paediatric Priorities in the Developing World.* London: Butterworths, 1973.

28. O'Malley, L.S. *Indian Caste Customs.* Calcutta: Rupa and Co., 1976.

29. Radbill, S.X. "A history of child abuse and infanticide," in *The Battered Child,* pp. 3–21. Edited by R.E. Helfer and C.H. Kempe. Chicago: University of Chicago Press, 1968.

30. Rajalakshmi, R. and Ramakrishnan, C.V. "Formulation and evaluation of meals based on locally available foods for young children." *World Review of Nutrition and Dietetics* 27 (1977):34–104.

31. Ramalingaswami, V. "Nutrition, cell biology and human development." *WHO Chronicle* 29 (August, 1975):306–312.

32. Roy Chaudhury, B. "Rural health care: Problems and priorities." *Journal of the Indian Medical Association* 70 (May, 1978):230.

33. Santhanakrishnan, B.R., Shetty, M.V., and Raju, V.B. "PITS Syndrome." *Indian Pediatrics* 10 (February, 1973):97–100.

34. Seth, V. and Ghai, O.P. "Mortality in protein-calorie malnutrition." *Indian Pediatrics* 9 (March, 1972):163–166.

35. Udani, P.M. et al. "Problem of tuberculosis in children in India—(epidemiology, morbidity, mortality and control programme)." *Indian Pediatrics* 13 (December, 1976):881–890.

36. Waterlow, J.C. "Classification and definition of PEM," in *Nutrition In Preventive Medicine,* pp. 530–555. Edited by G.H. Beaton and J.M. Bengoa. Geneva: WHO Monograph No. 62, 1976.

37. World Health Organization. *Human Development and Public Health,* Technical Report Series No. 485, Geneva, 1972.

**Part III
Spouse Abuse**

Introduction to Part III

The patriarchal hierarchy of most, if not all, modern societies has led to a culturally legitimized marital hierarchy in which wives are subordinate to their husbands. Violence against women is positively sanctioned by this social structure, resulting in humiliation, severe and/or frequent beatings, and possibly even death. The authors of the three articles in this section all discuss the importance of understanding the cultural context of the societies in which such violence takes place.

Gayford carried out the pioneering research on wife victimization in England. This article represents his most up-to-date thoughts on wife battering. Drawing on his prior research and the research of others, Gayford provides us with an overview of what is currently known about wife battering in England. He discusses research terminology common to the study of wife abuse, and highlights subtle yet important distinctions between definitions. In addition, he reviews the epidemiology and etiology of wife victimization. Some of the etiological factors Gayford sees as related to wife battering include: family background, education, employment, psychiatric history, alcohol and drug abuse, premarital violence, social conditions, sexual history, courtship, and marriage. Needless to say, some factors have been found to be better indicators of spousal violence than others. Gayford provides us with descriptions of the types and severity of injuries most often inflicted upon female victims of abuse. He also develops his own classification scheme on types of battered wives. Although he qualifies his classification scheme by saying any attempt to classify people is doomed to failure because of the complexity of human beings, Gayford nevertheless identifies three types of battered wives: the *inadequate wife,* the *highly competent wife,* and the *provocative wife.*

Mushanga's article on wife victimization in East and Central Africa bears remarkable similarities to the succeeding article by Dobash and Dobash which focuses on wife abuse in Scotland. Mushanga and the Dobashes agree that wives are the persons most frequently victimized within the family. Whether the violent episodes result in injury, as investigated by Dobash and Dobash, or in death, as examined by Mushanga, the home is a much more violent place for wives than husbands. The authors also agree that marriage customs, both in Africa and in Scotland, support the male point of view. Wife abuse is highly correlated with domination, control, and chastisement of women due to the inferior positions of wives. Mushanga further demonstrates the importance of the relationship between cultural legitimacy and extent of spousal violence by showing that in African societies where abuse is *not* positively sanctioned, the rates of wife victimization tend to be lower than in African societies where violence against wives is positively sanctioned.

9

Battered Wives

J.J. Gayford

Erin Pizzey[30] started her campaign on behalf of battered wives in 1971 and not only exploded the myth that women liked or desired the abuse they received from violent men but also brought home the horror and gravity of the situation. It may have been more convenient to believe this falsehood in the same way as battered babies were explained in quasi-metabolic and haematological terms until Kempe et al[23] shocked considered opinion into accepting reality. Very soon authors such as Radbill[31] were able to look back through history and see the atrocious ways in which some adults have treated children. In the same way Gayford[12,13] and May[27] have traced how, throughout recorded history and no doubt before, some men have abused their wives in violent ways.

At intervals throughout English history there have been notable people who have raised their voices against wife beating.[42] Documentary evidence of marital violence is more complete from the 19th century onwards.[3] There is a marked similarity between the emotive speeches in the House of Commons 100 years ago[20] which resulted in a Parliamentary Commission and the more recent speeches in the House of Commons which resulted in a Select Committee on Violence in Marriage.[38]

Following the Parliamentary Commission of 1875 there was a series of law reforms such as the Women's Property Act, 1882, the Matrimonial Causes Act, 1884, and even the Summary Jurisdiction (Married Women) Act, 1895, all of which attempted in a limited way to improve the lot of the married woman. The effects of the Select Committee on Violence in Marriage[38] are only just beginning to be seen. Gill and Coote[17] have given a brief account of how battered wives can use the law to protect themselves and extricate themselves from their predicament.

There is certainly a heightened awareness of marital violence with the appearance of a number of books on the subject: Gelles[16] and Steinmetz and Strauss[41] from the USA have contributed as have Borland,[2] Martin, [26] Mitchell,[28] and Renvoize[32] from the UK.

Terminology

Aggression and violence: Gunn[19] made the point that although aggression and violence are often used as interchangeable words there is a subtle

Reprinted with permission from the *British Journal of Hospital Medicine* (November), J.J. Gayford, "Battered wives," 1979, pp. 496–503, Hospital Medicine Publications.

distinction. Aggression is an unprovoked attack whereas violence is the exercise of physical force so as to inflict injury or damage to person or property. Thus aggression may be verbal but violence is always physical; aggression can be constructive but violence is always physically damaging. Aggressive words and physical violence may be used together in a row between two people, but words may also be used as a substitute for violence or violence may be used where words fail and control is lost. It is even possible to have a passive form of aggression, which can be provocative and may be reciprocated with violence. The role of the wife as provocateur is discussed by Snell et al.[40]

Marital or conjugal violence: In violence between spouses one party may be the attacker and the other the victim or both may attack each other. The degree of physical assault may be trivial or serious, the duration of the attack may be short or prolonged, and weapons may be used. Usually the male is stronger and is only the victim when this physical advantage is negated by use of weapons or, more frequently if he refrains from using his full strength. Very occasionally the male may be physically disadvantaged by disease but more commonly by drugs or so much alcohol that he is nearly unconscious.

It is rare for the man to really be the victim and once the male releases his full physical force without inhibition and even resorts to weapons, few women stand a chance. Scott[37] points out that if the victim is the weaker party he is subjected to multiple blows; if he is the stronger party he has to be felled with a single blow or the tables will be turned.

Battered: This is an emotive term that implies that repeated blows are struck in one direction with one party very much the attacker and the other the victim.

Battered wife: This term should be reserved for a woman who has been subjected to severe, repeated, deliberate, and demonstrable physical injury from her marital partner.[9] One blow does not make a battered wife, no matter how serious it is or even if it is fatal. It is the fact that the attacks are repeated and the blows multiple that constitutes the battering and this eventually leads to a dangerous situation.

Women may attack men and with the aid of weapons may kill them, but it is very rare indeed for them to batter men and then generally only under the circumstances discussed.

Tortured wife: This is a highly emotive term that was introduced by Cobbe.[3] If it is to be used at all it is best reserved for women who are subjected to cold calculated attacks that may have a sadistic element. This is absent in most cases of battered wives.

Family violence: This covers all types of violence within the family including child abuse (battered baby), marital violence of all the types described, and abuse of usually aged parents by their children.

Epidemiology

For every battered wife who presents for professional help or takes refuge in a hostel for battered wives, there are many others who hide their injuries or, when forced to seek medical help, give a spurious reason for their condition. Thus epidemiology becomes virtually impossible and all estimates are extremely inaccurate. Marsden and Owens[25] confirmed an incidence of one in 500 marriages in the Colchester area but felt that this was an underestimate because there were other known cases who were not prepared to be included in their survey. Estimates from the Samaritans and the Citizens' Advice Bureaux have been steadily rising from the meagre figure of 3 per cent of enquiries that was claimed in 1972. Politicians are bolder and prepared to claim a national incidence of 50,000 a year[21] but this can only be an inspired guess or an extrapolation from other data which allows for planning.

Aetiology

Cobbe[3] claimed that wife battering was caused by alcoholic intoxication, heteropathy, jealousy, and friction due to overcrowding and social deprivation. Heteropathy was defined as the opposite of sympathy, where the sight of pain and suffering created a desire to destroy rather than to help. Nearly 100 years later the Royal College of Psychiatrists presented to the DHSS a report on battered wives in which they suggested the same factors minus heteropathy and added immature or psychopathic personality, cultural factors, and drug abuse. However they thought that most psychotic disorders had little part to play.[36] They agreed with the Royal Scottish Society for the Prevention of Cruelty to Children[33] that there was an overlap with child abuse and a background of family violence.

Gayford[15] reviewed the aetiological factors as seen from his study of 100 battered wives. Analytical psychodynamic hypotheses have been provided by Schultz[34] and Snell et al.[40] which either project the blame onto the relationship between the husband and his mother or claim that the wife herself is really the instigator of the violence. Faulk[7] concluded that men who are violent to their wives for the first time after the age of 40 are more likely to be suffering from a psychotic disorder and those in the younger age-group are more likely to be psychopathic.

The following is presented as an outline of some of the aetiological factors.[13,15]

Family background: About 40 per cent of the men were exposed to violence during their childhood, compared with about a quarter of the women who witnessed violence between parents or were subjected to parental violence. More than a third of women were deprived of one or both parents before the age of 15 and over a quarter of women had to share their parents with at least five siblings. Both immigrant men and women from the Republic of Ireland and the West Indies appeared to be over-represented. All social classes were included.

Education and employment: In many cases women projected themselves as better educated than their male partners and backed this up with examination successes in a third of case histories. An overlapping third went on to further education after leaving school. Again, about a third of women had good work records, staying in a job for more than 3 years, with another overlapping third gaining satisfaction from their work; 14 per cent started training as nurses or teachers. About half the men had no employment problems, but a third were frequently out of work.

Psychiatric history: Nearly half the women had received a psychiatric consultation at some stage in their lives, but most of these were after the violence had started. Almost three quarters of battered wives had been prescribed antidepressants or tranquilizers by their GPs and over a third had made suicide attempts, again usually after the violence had started. It would appear that in only a few cases did the psychiatric disorder precede the marital violence and could truly be called an aetiological factor. An important clinical point made is that when most of the women presented to a GP, a casualty department, or a psychiatrist, the diagnosis was obscured in the majority of cases.

Alcohol and drug abuse: Heavy drinking and drunkenness appear to be major problems among the husbands of battered wives in three quarters of cases. In over 40 per cent of cases violence only occurred when the husband was drunk. Between 10–20 per cent of women went through a heavy-drinking phase, some with their husbands and others as a means of relieving distress caused indirectly by the violence. Alcoholism appears to be a major problem in men who batter their wives, but only a handful of women are battered because of their drinking. It would appear that women are more likely to abuse drugs than their violent husbands; most of these drugs would be obtained on prescription but in neither party did it appear to be a major cause of violence.

Morbid jealousy (Othello syndrome): Two thirds of battered women claimed that their husbands showed signs of jealousy and this seems to be the major aetiological factor. It has to be considered together with the promiscuity of either party and excessive drinking in the man. There is no doubt that some of the men want a very close exclusive type of relationship with their wives hardly speaking to members of the opposite sex. Indeed these poor women cannot win because any relationship with their own sex is projected as a sign of lesbianism. Accounts of violence being inflicted to extract confessions were encountered.

Premarital violence: A quarter of women reported that violence started before marriage or cohabitation. It would appear that if a woman is prepared to continue a relationship with a man who is violent to her before marriage, she is in danger of this violence being repeated after marriage when some of the traditional courtship respect may have lapsed.

Sexual history, courtship, and marriage: Nearly one in 10 battered wives seemed to have been involved in an incestuous relationship. Almost a quarter of the women claimed that they had been raped (relationships with husbands and cohabitees were excluded). The conclusion from these facts is that not an insignificant number of battered wives have experienced emotionally disturbing sexual relationships, most of whom seem to tolerate this without recourse to legal proceedings.

Less than a quarter of women went through the traditional courtship, including engagement, before marriage. The majority of women had regular sexual relationships before marriage or cohabitation, and only 2 per cent routinely used contraception. The mean age of marriage or cohabitation was 20.3 years (sd $\pm$ 3.2), with about 10 per cent doing so before their 18th birthday. Sixty per cent of women were pregnant before marriage or cohabitation and 15 per cent of these pregnancies were not by the man whom they subsequently married or with whom they cohabitated.

More than a quarter of women were in their second marital relationship, over half of the first relationships having ended due to violence. More of the men (over a third) had been involved in previous relationships of which well over half had ended due to violence. Men and women who have been in previously violent relationships seem to be in danger of entering further similar relationships: this is because men have a propensity to violence and women spend their social lives in a violent subculture with exposure to the company of latently violent men, desperately seeking further relationships. Such men are prepared to accept women who have had violent marriages, along with their children who are almost inevitably disturbed.

Promiscuity with extramarital sexual relationships plays a part in precipitating jealousy and may also lead to violence directly or indirectly. Almost one woman in five admitted to extramarital affairs but nearly half the men were accused of the same activity.

It is difficult to estimate the extent to which failure in marital sexual relationships was responsible for frustration and violence. A quarter of women claimed that they had never experienced sexual enjoyment at any time during the relationship. As the violence developed, more women failed to enjoy sexual relationships, but a surprising number of women had no complaint about this aspect of their marriage.

There was no real evidence that sadism on the part of the men or masochism on the part of the women played any part in the violence. Scott[36] also agreed with this, which suggests that the reality of marital violence destroys any enjoyment of sadomasochistic fantasy. Homosexuality of either sex did not appear to be an important factor, while absent completely in the men, only isolated cases of facultative lesbianism were found in the women at an all-female hostel.

Social conditions: The importance of poverty and poor housing conditions in the aetiology of marital violence is also difficult to estimate. Certainly a quarter of the women had their poverty made worse and more unpredictable by heavy gambling by their husbands. Few complained of poverty unless pressed, but for many social security had become a fact of life. Crowded housing conditions must have made matters worse although the converse does not appear to prevent marital violence.

Overlap with child abuse: There is now little doubt that there is an overlap between child abuse and wife battering; this was suggested by Scott[36] and confirmed by the Royal Scottish Society for the Prevention of Cruelty to Children.[33] About a third of women admitted that in frustration, often after they themselves had been subjected to violence from their husbands, they have hit their children much harder than they should or in an uncontrolled manner. In half the cases it appeared that the husbands extended their violence to the children and this was frequently the factor that precipitated the women into leaving the marital home.

Presentation

The physical effects of men losing control and violently assaulting their wives have been studied by Fonseka[8] who looked at radiological evidence of injuries, and by Gayford[9,10,13] who studied the injuries found on women at a refuge for battered wives. Levine[24] and Dewsbury[4] studied marital violence as seen in general practice. The forensic aspect of women who have been killed by their husbands is a completely different subject and is not discussed.

Injuries vary considerably from the trivial to the serious. The types that may be seen in a casualty department are described below. As with battered babies, presentation for treatment is often delayed and the story of how the injury was received may be fabricated to hide the truth. Not infrequently women try to conceal injuries, staying indoors until physical signs have subsided. Alternatively they may be accompanied by their husbands who give the account of the events, refuse to be separated from their wives, and remove them from medical care as soon as possible often against medical advice. Attempted suicides may present in the same way and alarming accounts have been given of women being kept at home for a couple of days in an unconscious or semiconscious state.

Most injuries are found on the head and the neck, with a periorbital haematoma being the commonest. When seen early (within 24 hours) the eye is swollen and closed and there may be an associated subconjunctival haemorrhage. If the blow was heavy, that is inflicted with a weapon or by the patient being kicked, the bruising extends into the malar region. Most frequently, injuries are seen late when swelling has subsided. Lacerations around the eyes are quite common, the usual mode of attack being with the fists often with rings on the fingers. Swelling of the lips with lacerations and fractures of the teeth are not infrequent. Injury to the nose with possible fracture is also fairly commonplace. Trauma above the hair-line of the scalp is said to be inflicted deliberately in the more calculated attacks that are designed to cause injury with little physical signs. Strangulation attempts are claimed by about 20 per cent of women but there are usually few signs, although the women given an alarming description of sudden loss of consciousness which suggests that they were subjected to bilateral carotid compression.

Bruising around the arms and wrists is a sign that the woman has been restrained but does not always indicate that the man was the aggressor. The appearance of much deeper bruising is thought to imply that she was kicked or hit with a weapon. Occasionally women have been thrown about a room with painful injuries to the shoulder. Ribs are frequently fractured, usually when the victim was kicked while lying on the ground, and injuries to the lumbar sacral region generally occur in the same way. As long ago as 1878 Cobbe described the horrific case of a man jumping on a pregnant woman's abdomen, and regrettably there are still similar accounts of injury to the abdomen.

Burns and scalds usually occur when the violence takes place in the kitchen and hot utensils have been used in the attack. Fractures other than those of the nose, ribs, and teeth are only rarely seen and are a sign of a more serious sustained attack.

For the most part the picture is one of a man completely losing control and hitting his wife repeatedly with his fists, kicking her, and using any available weapon as he buffets her about the room. The attack is not usually premeditated but when it is the injuries, although not necessarily more severe, have more sinister connotations and it is obvious that the woman has been subjected to a type of torture. Examples of this are women who have been burned with cigarettes, or worse still, a hot poker; also, some women have had initials carved on their breasts.[4]

After the event the man may have amnesia, or in shame may wish to blot out the memory. There is no doubt that there is a loss of control similar to that in the episodic dyscontrol syndrome.[1] Alternatively, the events are followed by profound remorse with the husband trying to make up for the damage by exemplary conduct.

Types of Battered Wife

It would be untrue to say that any man can batter his wife but as Faulk[7] found in a small sample there are a variety of types of men in prison for this offence. It would be equally untrue to say that any woman can become a battered wife although several types have been described.[11] Any attempt to classify people is rightly doomed to failure because human beings are too complex to be "pigeon-holed". In practice a battered wife may have various characteristics of the types described below—it is helpful to list them under headings.

Inadequate wife: It is often difficult to decide how much of the inadequacy has been precipitated by the repeated episodes of violence; an inadequate woman becomes more so under these circumstances. However, she is able to live under adversity and to tolerate difficult situations much longer than most people. She was brought up to this and her current family pattern is only a repetition of what she experienced in childhood. Social workers have despaired of helping this type of family, often labelled as "problem families" and described by Tonge et al.[43] as "families without hope".

This type of inadequate woman was probably victimized at school where she had a poor record in both attendance and achievement. One of her chances to leave home was through marriage and the only type of man who would tolerate her family background was somebody brought up in similar circumstances. Marriage tended to be early, often precipitated by pregnancy. Further children followed and accommodation was always a problem.

Her husband is unlikely to have a good work record and this may have been punctuated by prison sentences, with income further reduced by drinking and possibly gambling. An overlap with child abuse is not an infrequent complication of the family's problems. Psychiatric help has occasionally been sought but is unlikely to yield encouraging results. Treatment with antidepressants or tranquilizers can lead to suicide attempts.

It goes without saying that this type of battered wife is the most difficult to help; however, she seems to fare better in one of the Women's Aid hostels than with conventional psychiatric and social care. In other words she needs to be taken into total care with her children and to be surrounded by other women who can act as surrogate mothers to her children when required. In this way she gradually learns, but it is a lengthy process which takes many years and may be punctuated by abortive attempts at reconcilation with her husband.

There is a particular type of inadequate woman who is subjected to the most cruel and prolonged violence if she has married a bullying man. Unfortunate cases of both herself and the children being burned with cigarettes have been seen. She may be the victim of acts of sexual degradation that are sickening and have nothing to do with sex. The only thing that needs to be said about such acts is that they are not necessarily sadistic but those of a drunken man showing his disgust after he has been sexually refused. There is no doubt that this type of woman and her children need to be removed from such a situation and handled with care and consideration while legal proceedings take place. Both she and her children will need considerable rehabilitation.

Highly competent wife: At first it is difficult to see how this type of woman becomes a battered wife. She has often been brought up in a protective environment, has had a good education, and holds a responsible job. Intellectually she is frequently her husband's superior, forcing him to rely on her for help in his career. The withdrawal of this help leaves him in a vulnerable position. Her marriage may have caused a rift between her family and herself, making it difficult or embarrassing to accept help from them when there is a crisis due to violence. This type of woman with a middle-class background was studied in the USA by Snell et al.[40] when she and her husband presented for psychiatric help. They saw such women as aggressive and efficient with the husband occasionally having to assert himself, usually when his inhibitions had been removed by alcohol. Such a view was also expressed by Whitehurst[44] who found similar middle-class families who could be taught to suppress violence for fear of public disapproval and loss of social status.

It is certainly this type of woman who presents with the hope of some psychotherapeutic intervention. If this is to be undertaken alcoholism and morbid jealousy should be excluded and a framework devised by which violence cannot bring about a rewarding situation for the husband. Most feminists would be highly critical of male-orientated psychoanalytical ideas of the woman needing to become more submissive in order to be less provocative to a male with a low frustration tolerance. Even so there are women who blame themselves for precipitating the violence, especially when they are experiencing premenstrual tension.

Provocative wife: There are many ways in which women can be provocative and so cause friction in a marital relationship. Factors such as inadequacy and overcontrol have already been discussed. Another of the more obvious causes is sexual provocation which when coupled with morbid jealousy is a most dangerous combination.[39] It has been known to lead to homicide or, more accurately, uxoricide.[29]

This type of woman has always enjoyed the company of the opposite sex, even in childhood. Not only does she know how to seek attention but also often enjoys the game of offsetting one man against another. She is generally vivacious and energetic, with many of the qualities of the stimulus seeker who is constantly looking for excitement. This is one of the few types of women who will try to hit back in violent episodes, but she also soon learns that when a man has completely lost his temper a woman is no physical match for him. Her husband may be an exciting man in her eyes and there is a tendency towards frequent separations and reconciliations. Both she and her husband tend to have extramarital sexual relationships, but nevertheless they often have an exciting sexual relationship within the marriage in spite of the violence.

When trying to help this type of woman it is important to remember that she needs excitement. Placed in a quiet hostel when the violence has become too much, or moved to a bed-sitter, she will seek out her violent husband or at least let him know where she can be found. Alternatively she will find a new boyfriend who will have many of the qualities of her violent husband. At Chiswick Women's Aid this type of woman is invaluable in helping other women in crises and in doing this she gains the excitement she desires without endangering herself. Eventually she tires of the excitement and seeks a more peaceful domestic life.

Long-standing case: Twenty per cent of women seen by Gayford in 1973—74 had experienced violence for more than 10 years.[9] This was at a time when hostels were only just becoming available and there were few places to which women could escape. Violence has become a way of life for this type of woman and she may well have experienced similar treatment from her father. There is a sad air of resignation; if she did not leave home when her children left, she stayed for the sake of possessions or pets or due to an inability to make a new way of life in middle age. If her husband is a heavy drinker, drunkenness occurs more quickly and his physical health starts to deteriorate. As a result of this the physical damage lessens and eventually he becomes a rather pathetic dependent old man.

Cases complicated by alcohol, drugs, and a psychiatric history: Occasionally, battered women who drink heavily themselves or abuse drugs join those with a psychiatric history in hospital. In all these cases it is difficult to determine which came first, the violence or the disorder, but in many the drug and alcohol abuse or the psychiatric problems continue after there has been a separation from the violent man. Battered wives who abuse alcohol frequently tend to have a family history of alcoholism or a husband with drinking problems. There is overlap between the types of women who abuse alcohol and those who abuse drugs. Both tend to suffer from other psychotic disorders such as anxiety or recurrent depression.

Violent wife: Very few women (8 per cent) regularly tried to hit back when their husbands were violent, most having learned that this only accelerated the violence and that they usually came off worse. It is strange how strong women often have even stronger husbands. Fortunately the type of woman who is frequently involved in fights with other women is rare. Less than 5 per cent of battered wives appear to be involved in a variety of problems which can end in extramarital violence. This type of woman may have a very violent husband and both may have been involved in conflicts with the law. She may be part of a drug-taking heavy-drinking set and two cases seen had lesbian tendencies.

Pseudo-battered wife: Following the publicity of the phenomenon of the battered wife there have been a few cases in which delusions of marital violence have become part of the repertoire of the paranoid schizophrenic. More commonly women claim that they have been battered because they wish to end their marriages and discredit their husbands. This type of woman does not stay long at a busy overcrowded hostel for battered wives. She can rarely present any direct evidence of the violence, but gives an account that may trap the inexperienced or the unwary.

Investigation and Management

Intervention with psychotherapy should be tried only when violence has been minimal or isolated. Professional middle-class couples who value their social reputation have a behavioral restraint readily available. Cases in which there is a history of drug or alcohol abuse by either party are best treated for this disability first. Violent men are coming forward for help only gradually; this is mainly because they want to keep their wives, but generally on their own terms. Men with sudden explosive rage need to be fully investigated including EEG studies.[6] When violence occurs for the first time late in life, loss of control due to dementing processes must be excluded.

Periodic depressive episodes especially those with an anxiety component may cause some people to be very irritable; in the woman this can be a provocative factor and in the man it may precipitate violence. Claims of schizophrenia in the man are far more common than cases actually substantiated. Anxiety and especially agoraphobia in battered wives are not uncommonly seen and some behavioral treatment of the agoraphobia may be beneficial. Cases in which there is an element of morbid jealousy need to be handled with great care and most would see this as a sign that the parties should seek separation. Even this may not be an end of the problem because not infrequently this type of jealous man may keep his former wife under surveillance after divorce. He may take exception to her attempting new relationships and even demand what he still considers to be his conjugal rights.

It is extremely common for children of battered wives to suffer from behavioral disturbances including bed-wetting, school refusal, theft, and vandalism. Few battered wives are able to cope with these disorders. Some of the temper tantrums seen in these children are quite frightening to behold and may exclude them from most organizations for children. Children from these families often need to be taken into care, but their mothers may resent this and compensate their loss by initiating a further pregnancy.

When a woman has decided to take legal action (either criminal or civil) against her husband, she will find it an almost impossible task to continue living under the same roof while the legal proceedings reach their conclusion. The threat of further violence has deterred many women from going ahead. More commonly there is a genuine ambivalence over the whole matter which may swing each way a number of times before a final decision is reached.

Hostels for battered wives have only recently become available.[22] These are run by voluntary organizations under the general term of Women's Aid and can provide more than just shelter. Most offer a counseling service that includes access to a solicitor who has the necessary skills and is prepared to represent the women under legal aid.

There are two main types of hostel, the open door and the restricted admission. The open-door hostels, of which the most famous is Chiswick Women's Aid founded by Erin Pizzey, take women and children who present no matter where they originate from or what time of day or night they arrive. These hostels tend to be crowded and attract the most severe cases with their disturbed children. There is a central crisis refuge that takes all new cases, which is supported by facilities for children and secondary hostels where women and children may reside on a long-term basis. The restricted-admission hostels tend not to publicize their addresses and admission has to be made through specific and rather secret channels. Most are small houses where only a given number of women and children can be accommodated in family rooms. They tend to be more comfortable and occasionally house women who would not fit the definition of a battered wife. The Select Committee on Violence in Marriage[38] requested the Department of the Environment to encourage local authorities or voluntary organizations to provide refuges on the basis of one family place per 10,000 of the population.

The rehabilitation of women and children is a long and complicated process which may be hindered if the battered wife seeks a new relationship with another man of a similar type. At a mean age of 31, with, on average, two disturbed children, most battered wives have difficulty in finding stable partners. It is a sad fact that many of their children will take marital violence into the next generation. Cases have been seen where this condition has passed through three generations.

The Dynamics of Violence in Marriage

Behavioral theory suggests that violence is a learned pattern of behavior.[35] Analytical theory tends to equate aggression and violence and postulates that this is always preceded by frustration.[5] Marital violence, like most real violent situations, substantiates some elements of both theories but raises questions about others. Gorney[18] argued that with increased intensity of emotional feeling there is a greater liability of eruption into violence. The psychodynamics of marital violence are postulated and discussed fairly fully by Snell et al.,[40] Faulk,[7] and Gayford.[13,14]

The relationship between battered wives and their husbands is intense, with both parties striving to keep it alive in spite of the obvious failings. If this were not so, there would simply be a separation between the two parties. Both have made some investment in the relationship and see themselves losing if they are the ones to pull out, even if that loss will only be material. Gayford[10] showed that only a third of women had no positive feelings for their husbands.

Both parties need to be considered in terms of their frustration tolerance which can be lowered by external social factors or internal psychological and physical factors. The focus falls on the husband's frustration tolerance which, when exhausted, will be the critical factor. Some men will never be violent; this is not their way of dealing with situations. Others have learned from experience, which may include the example of their parents, that violence appears to solve problems where other ways fail. This has to be associated with some blunting of the perception of what happens to general relationships when violence erupts.

Both parties can be provocative, but in this article the focus is on the wife as the victim. Women vary a great deal in their provocative qualities and these may be affected by physical, psychological, and social situations. If a woman of low provocation is paired with a man of high frustration tolerance, violence is highly unlikely; even if a highly provocative woman is paired with this same type of man with high frustration tolerance, violence is unlikely but divorce is quite possible. The problem of violence starts when a man with low frustration tolerance is paired with a highly provocative woman; this is what happens in violent marriages.

Many women report the feeling of tension rising before violence erupts. In some cases this may take only minutes, but others have described this feeling building up for days. Alcohol is very important in this equation because it removes inhibitions and allows violence to erupt.

Less than 20 per cent of battered wives are not legally married but they are trapped in the relationship by the same factors as the wedded woman, namely the difficulty in leaving because of children. It is rare for childless women to present because they somehow manage to escape the full severity of the attack. All ages of adult women present; usually battered wives are in their late 20s and early 30s, although older women are not immune. By the time women have found it necessary to take refuge in a hostel for battered wives they have generally been in the marital relationship for some years.

References

1. Bach-Y-Rita, G., Lion, J.R., Climent, C.E., and Ervin, F.R. "Episodic dyscontrol: A study of 130 violent patients." *American Journal of Psychiatry* 127 (1971):1473–1478.

2. Borland, M. (ed.) *Violence in the Family.* England: Manchester University Press, 1976.

3. Cobbe, F.P. "Wife torture in England." *The Contemporary Review* 32 (1878):57–87.

4. Dewsbury, A.R. "Battered wives. Family violence seen in general practice." *Royal Society of Health Journal* 95 (December, 1975):290–294.

5. Dollard, J. et al. *Frustration and Aggression.* Institute of Human Relations, Yale University, 1944.

6. Elliott, F.A. "The neurology of explosive rage. The dyscontrol syndrome." *Practitioner* 217 (July, 1976):51–60.

7. Faulk, M. "Men who assault their wives." *Medicine, Science and Law* 14 (July, 1974):180–183.

8. Fonseka, S. "A study of wife-beating in the Camberwall area." *British Journal of Clinical Practice* 28 (December, 1974):400–402.

9. Gayford, J.J. "Wife battering: A preliminary survey of 100 cases," *British Medical Journal* 1 (January, 1975):194–197.

10. Gayford, J.J. "Battered wives." *Medicine Science and Law* 15 (October, 1975):237–245.

11. Gayford, J.J. "Ten types of battered wives." *Welfare Officer* 25 (1976): 5–9.

12. Gayford, J.J. "Battered wives one hundred years ago." *Practitioner* 219 (July, 1977):122–128.

13. Gayford, J.J. Battered wives: The study of the Aetiology and psychosocial effects among one hundred women. MD Thesis, University of London, 1978.

14. Gayford, J.J. "Battered wives," in *Violence and the Family,* pp. 19–39. Edited by J.P. Martin. Chichester: John Wiley, 1978.

15. Gayford, J.J. "The aetiology of repeated serious physical assaults by husbands on wives (wife beating)". *Medicine, Science and the Law* 19 (January, 1979):19–24.

16. Gelles, R.J. *The Violent Home: A Study of Physical Aggression between Husbands and Wives.* London: Sage, 1972.

17. Gill, T. and Coote, A. *Battered Women: How to use the Law.* London: Cobden Trust, 1975.

18. Gorney, R. "Interpersonal intensity, competition, and synergy: Determinants of achievement, aggression, and mental illness." *American Journal of Psychiatry* 128 (October, 1971):436–445.

19. Gunn, J.C. *Violence in Human Society.* London: David and Charles, 1973.

20. Hansard, *Criminal Law; Assaults on Women.* Resolution 219, 18 May (1874):396.

21. Hansard, Speech by Jack Ashley MP, 17 July (1973):218.

22. Harrison, P. "Refugees for wives." *New Society* 34(684, 1975):361–364.

23. Kempe, C.H. et al. "The battered child syndrome." *Journal of the American Medical Association* 181 (July, 1962):17–24.

24. Levine, M.B. "Interparental violence and its effect on the children: A study of 50 families in general practice." *Medicine, Science and Law* 15 (July, 1975):172–176.

25. Marsden, D. and Owens, D. "Jeckyll and Hyde marriages." *New*

Society 32(657, 1975):333–335.

26. Martin, J.P. (ed.) *Violence and the Family.* Chichester: John Wiley, 1978.

27. May, M. "Violence in the family: An historical perspective," in *Violence and the Family,* pp. 135–167. Edited by J.P. Martin. Chichester: John Wiley, 1978.

28. Mitchell, A.R.K. *Violence in the Family.* Hove: Wayland Publishers, 1978.

29. Perdue, W.C. "A preliminary investigation into uxoricide." *Diseases of the Nervous System* 27 (December, 1966):808–811.

30. Pizzey, E. *Scream Quietly or the Neighbors Will Hear.* Harmondsworth: Penguin, 1974.

31. Radbill, S.X. "A history of child abuse and infanticide," in *The Battered Child,* pp. 3–17. Edited by R.E. Helfer and C.H. Kempe. USA: University of Chicago Press, 1974.

32. Renvoize, J. *Web of Violence: A Study of Family Violence.* London: Routledge and Kegan Paul, 1978.

33. Royal Scottish Society for Prevention of Cruelty to Children. *Battered Wives Survey.* 1974.

34. Schultz, L.G. "The wife assaulter." *Journal of Social Therapy* 6(2, 1960):103–112.

35. Scott, J.P. *Aggression.* USA: University of Chicago Press, 1958.

36. Scott, P.D. "Battered wives." *British Journal of Psychiatry* 125 (November, 1974):433–441.

37. Scott, P.D. "Non-accidental injury in children. Memorandum of evidence to the Parliamentary Select Committee on Violence in the Family." *British Journal of Psychiatry* 131 (October, 1977):366–380.

38. Select Committee on Violence in Marriage HC55311.HMSO, London, 1975.

39. Shephard, M. "Morbid jealousy: Some clinical and social aspects of a psychiatric symptom." *Journal of Mental Science* 107 (July, 1961):687–753.

40. Snell, J.E., Rosenwald, R.J., and Robey, A. "The wifebeater's wife: A study of family interaction." *Archives of General Psychiatry* 11 (August, 1964):107–112.

41. Steinmetz, S.K. and Straus, M.A. (eds.) *Violence in the Family.* New York: Dodd, Mead and Company, 1974.

42. Stone, L. *The Family, Sex and Marriage in England 1500–1800.* London, Weidenfeld and Nicolson, 1977.

43. Tonge, W.L., James, D.S., and Hillam, S.M. *British Journal of Psychiatry,* Special Publication No. 11, 1975.

44. Whitehurst, R.N. "Violence in husband-wife interaction," in *Violence in the Family,* pp. 75–82. Edited by S.K. Steinmetz and M.A. Straus. New York: Dodd, Mead, and Company, 1974.

10 Wife Victimization in East and Central Africa

Tibamanya mwene Mushanga

Data on Wife Victimization

In some of the communities in East and Central Africa the wife is the most often victimized and most often killed person within the immediate domestic group. Different cultures have different ways of resolving crises; some stress the use of violence while others require that such crisis situations and conflict be resolved in ways other than violent ones.

The data used in this paper were collected by different researchers at different times and from different African societies. Data from Ankole, Kigezi, and Toro districts in the Western province of Uganda as well as those referred to as extra sample were collected by the author and relate to the 12-year period from 1955 to 1968 inclusive. The extra sample data refer to cases of criminal homicide that were collected from other areas of Uganda outside the Western province.[5] Data on the Alur people of north Uganda were collected by Southall and cover a 10-year period from 1945 to 1954 inclusive. Data for the Abasoga of Western Uganda were collected by L.A. and M.C. Fallers for the years 1952 to 1954. Data for Abanyoro of Western Uganda were collected by J.H.M. Beattie and cover a period of over 20 years up to 1955. Data on the Bagisu of Eastern Uganda were collected by Jean La Fontaine for 1948 to 1954 inclusive. A total of seven ethnic groups are taken from Uganda, six of whom are the 'Bantu' stock and only the Alur belong to the 'Nilotic' group of people.

From Kenya, data were collected on the Abaluhya of Western Kenya by Paul Bohannan for the years 1949 and 1954. Data on the Joluo, also of Western Kenya, were collected by G.M. Wilson before 1955. Data on the last group of people, the Tiv, a semi-Bantu people who live in central Nigeria in West Africa, were collected by Bohannan and cover 1949–1955. All of these studies are found in a book on homicide and suicide edited by Bohannan.[2] Data for a small sample referred to as Kamiti were collected by the author at Kamiti Maximum Prison in Kenya and do not represent any single ethnic group of people within the Republic of Kenya.[6]

The following table shows the frequency of victimization of wives among these communities in comparison with eight other relations within the family.

Table 10-1
Victimization of Wives among Selected Communities

Group	Fa*	Mo	Bro	Si	Wi	Hus	Da	So	Total	% of wife as victim
Ankole	4	3	10	—	10	5	4	6	42	23.1
Kigezi	7	3	1	—	6	4	4	9	34	17
Toro	1	—	9	—	13	2	—	1	26	50
Extra sample	4	2	5	1	14	6	1	7	40	35
Alur	1	—	2	—	2	—	—	—	5	40
Abasoga	1	—	1	—	39	—	—	—	41	95
Abanyoro	1	—	1	—	8	—	—	—	10	80
Abaluhya	3	—	4	—	5	—	—	1	13	38
Luo	—	—	1	—	6	—	—	—	7	85
Bagisu	7	—	5	—	7	4	—	—	23	35
Tiv	—	—	7	—	8	1	—	—	16	50
Kamiti sample	5	—	5	—	7	—	1	3	21	33.5
Total	34	8	51	1	125	22	10	27	278	44.5

*Fa = Father, Mo = Mother, Bro = Brother, Si = Sister, Wi = Wife, Hus = Husband, Da = Daughter, and So = Son.

Table 10-1 shows that the wife is the most victimized person within the family in all the groups considered except the Abakiga people (shown as Kigezi—the name of their homeland—in the table). The Abatero of Toro district, the Abanyankore of Ankole district, and the Tiv of Nigeria have a high criminal homicide rate against the brother. The highest rate of wife victimization was by the Abasoga of Eastern Uganda. The table also shows that the sister is the least victimized person in the family of origin, although she is frequently victimized when she marries and becomes a wife.

Analysis and Explanations

The explanation of human violence presents a formidable task. Some believe that violence among human beings is an innate and therefore a biological and genetic trait—that in fact aggressive tendencies can be seen in infants when they cry, kick, and pull their hair. This theory has often been advanced to explain violence, brutality, murder, and general nastiness of African soldiers and regimes against fellow countrymen. But if this were true, violence would be the general characteristic of all soldiers and regimes the world over. The fact that different racial and ethnic groups all over the world show marked differences in the use of violence in settling interpersonal conflicts may indicate that biology plays a relatively minor part in determining criminal homicide offenders, rapists, and other violent offenders. It also appears that if aggression is an innate trait common to all human beings, then its expression is largely determined by cultural and environmental factors most of which are beyond the individual's control. Thus an explanation of acts of violence must be sought not so much in the biology of the individual or of the group to which he or she belongs but in the culture of the individual violent offender's native group.

Numerous studies have shown that crime, and particularly violent crime, is predominantly a male activity. Wolfgang[11] reports that every study known confirms this fact. Numerous explanations have been given for this male supremacy in crime and violence, nearly all tending to name cultural values, role-playing, and expectations defined by given cultural group norms. These same studies show that those involved in acts of violence such as rape, assault, or homicide usually know each other or are related. Wolfgang found, as did Bensing and Schroeder, that homicide is usually an intraracial crime. [1,10] Violence is also an intra-sex activity. Men fight and kill men; rarely will males kill females. These facts appear to be common to all groups of people. Both of these factors—race and sex—show that criminal homicide results from other social interactional processes. That is, criminal homicide tends to occur within existing relationships.

The data as presented in the table reveal a third major observation; when violence erupts within the family group, the wife stands a much greater risk of being killed than any other family member.[9] The table shows that of 278 victims, 125 or 44.5 percent were wives. Factors that underlie this phenomenon must be sought within the processes of family life.

It is in the nuclear family that the individual looks for support, sympathy, comfort, and love. Each member of the family has his or her roles to play for the general well-being of the group. In some of these communities the roles attached to the status of 'wife,' 'husband,' or 'brother' involve obligations which, if not met, may anger another family member. The wife is usually the fulcrum of the family. Thus differential association becomes an important theory in explaining why the wife is the most common victim of intra-family homicide. Studies done in Uganda and Kenya in the last few years on criminal homicide show, in general, that violent homicide involving people who are related to each other tends to be the culmination of a series of episodes over a period of time rather than an abrupt eruption of violence, as is common among friends during a drinking session. The major factors of family conflicts are priority, frequency, duration, and intensity.[8]

Priority refers to how soon after the marriage the disputes and conflicts begin. This should show that the earlier the disputes begin, the more likely they are to lead to domestic disasters. The Abanyankore have a proverb saying that those who start quarrelling while they are preparing to build a house never live together. Disputes that start soon after marriage lead to either divorce, separation, or frequent fights which sometimes result in the death of either the wife, the husband, or other members of the family. It appears from the victims' ages that it is the young wife, perhaps married for a few years, that is likely to be killed rather than one who has been married for 10, 15 or more years.

Frequency refers to frequency of contact between members of the family in which a man has most frequent contact with his wife, not including small children. Violence is most likely to erupt if these frequent contacts are characterized by conflicts.

Duration refers to the time such frequent disputes have lasted. This may mean that cases of criminal homicide in which the victim is either the wife or the husband are most unlikely to result from single outbursts. The following case illustrates how prolonged conflicts may end in homicide:

> Zeinab and Hassan lived for several years in an unsuccessful marriage which Zeinab deeply resented because she had been forced to marry her cousin. Zeinab, now 30 years old, was married at a young age against her mother's wishes but with the approval of the rest of the family. Zeinab saw to it that the marriage was not a success and for many years she remained with her parents and resisted her husband's attempts to install her in his house. The two quarrelled frequently and once Zeinab's father had to intervene when Hassan complained of his wife's disobedience. One night the two had been drinking separately with friends and when they laid down for the night Hassan asked for sex but Zeinab refused, kicking him away. In a drunken rage he drew his knife and stabbed her while she did not resist. She died soon after. Hassan was found guilty of assault with a deadly weapon and was sentenced to 10 years imprisonment.[3]

The last factor in evaluating family conflict is intensity. In this context, intensity refers to the closeness of interpersonal relationship and also to psychological and emotional attachment between the conflicting individuals. The sexual relationship of husband and wife is an intense one characterized by jealousy and possessiveness. It is a highly emotionally charged relationship, reinforced by cultural values, which often breeds conflict.

Among the people of these communities, men victimize their wives for motives ranging from sexual infidelity to financial disputes, to chronic drunkenness, or suspicion of witchcraft. Some of these cultures, however, use strong negative sanctions against violence against wives by husbands. In Ankole, such a man risks losing his status and being subjected to ridicule and shame especially among his contemporaries and male relatives. In such societies, the annual rate of criminal homicide tends to be lower than in societies where violence against the wife is not regarded as any more heinous than that directed against any other member of the society. In Busoga (Eastern Uganda) where the rate of wife-killing appears to be extremely high, the explanation appears to be within the institution of marriage which has undergone an undesirable change. Temporary marriages seem to be replacing permanent, traditional marriage, and divorce, separation, desertion and suicide are on the increase. One informant said that there is no marriage in Busoga. Wives openly engage in extramarital relations with other men and this leads to family breakdown and very often to violence.

The Victim—Offender Relationship

At the sight of a victim of a violent crime, most spectators will give their unofficial verdicts against the offender. Few consider the victim's contribution to his or her own victimization. In the study of criminal homicide in Uganda mentioned above, it was found that the victim of a homicide could be partially or wholly to blame for his or her own death. Gonzalez has shown that frequently the victim of a crime will, consciously or unconsciously, create the conditions facilitating or favoring the commission of a crime.[4] Victims do facilitate their own deaths in many ways. Sometimes the victim invites the offender to kill her or she may use offensive and provocative language which may enrage the husband, as the following case shows:

> I found Malitina having sexual intercourse with Kisoke in his house. I shouted, "Kisoke" twice. I said, "Release her." Kisoke said very rude words to me. I said I would do something bad to you this day. I then set his house on fire. Malitina ran out and I caught her and said, "You, too, will suffer today." Kisoke had taken Malitina twice and seduced her. Malitina came back later that night and said I was too small for her, and I could eat her vagina. This annoyed me very much and I seized my panga and struck her. I only intended to punish her. I was very sorry for what I had done.[5]

In another case the deceased again was the wife of the accused. One night, the deceased complained that the accused was a very poor lover and compared very unfavorably in lovemaking with another man called Daudi. While so complaining she squeezed the accused's testicles. The accused got hold of her and strangled her to death. Sexual infidelity and suspicion are equally important in the genesis of conflict and violence. In some cases the matter is made worse when one or both of the partners is drunk.[7] The role of alcohol in these cases can be clearly illustrated by the following case:

> I was coming from drinking at Rwagara's home. It was at 1:00 p.m. I came together with Banjikira, Kuribuuza, and Mugara. When we reached the Kikunyu tree, I told Banjikira that I was going to Sentabire's with Mugara; then Mugara asked me to have sexual intercourse with him. I allowed him. We went into the bush and had sexual intercourse. He had sexual intercourse with me for one round; then my husband came and found us standing; he walked for a short time three paces; he then came back and stabbed me with a

spear in my ribs and pulled it out. When he came back, he found me lying down; he touched me to see if I had died. A man called Katondwe then came. That is my statement. (She died soon after making the statement.)[5]

In the cultural contexts of the groups under discussion, a wife would be asking for trouble if she engaged in extramarital sexual relationships, especially with men from clans other than the one to which her husband belongs. Even in such cases, a woman to be found in *in flagrante delicto* by her husband may cause an outburst of anger from him. However cases in which a man surprises his wife in bed with another man seem not be as frequent as cases of suspected infidelity.

Some cases of victim-precipitated homicides in which the wife is the victim result from direct invitation. In one case, a woman, wife of the accused, took a stick and began beating her husband while calling upon him to kill her. [2] In other cases, a woman may directly encourage her husband to hit her more by saying to him: "It was your father who knew how to beat; as for you, you are just playing with a stick." Cases also are on record in which wives get killed by taunting their husbands as being impotent.

In some cases a woman may actually be inviting trouble by persistently doing things contrary to the culturally defined ways of doing them. For example, a woman should not publicly insult her husband or her husband's father, mother, or brother. And a woman should not consciously or unconsciously let it be known that she is a witch or is capable of practicing magic and witchcraft against her husband or her husband's other wives and their children. In societies where ways of behavior are defined in terms of group culture, one risks his or her life by engaging in situations that may facilitate the eruption of violence. A woman who stages an argument with her husband in front of other people, especially when one or both have been drinking, stands a good risk of being a victim of violence. This is especially true among the less educated or uneducated and those who are unemployed or who are employed in the traditional sector of the economy, as cultivators, herdsmen, porters, cleaners and the like. These are the people who are orthodox in their views about the way things are and should be done. To them, wives are women whose roles are defined as those of procreation of children, cultivation of the fields, cooking, and general care of the family but, above all, to remain subservient to their husbands. These are the tradition-oriented men who will not want to hear any "nonsense" about "equality" between men and women.

Marriage customs among the majority of the African people support this male view. When a woman gets married, she physically moves from her father's home to that of her new husband after bridewealth (or brideprice) has been paid by the husband. Although African people never regarded the institution of brideprice as "buying" a wife, in a conflict situation an enraged man may say, "I bought you with my cows (money, etc.) and you stand there to . . . ?" In the same way a woman who is married without the payment of brideprice by her husband may say to her husband, "Why do you treat me like this? I will return to my parents; after all, you paid nothing for me."

It would appear that the new ideas about women's liberation in communities that are generally traditional may create situations in which the wife may directly or indirectly bring about her own death. This may happen as a result of a woman's attempt to assert her own rights, which may conflict with cultural patterns of behavior and socially accepted responses of a wife towards her husband. Women's liberation movements and ideas about such liberation appear to be generally acceptable to the educated and the well-to-do men of the young generations but remain quite alien and utterly unacceptable to the uneducated and the tradition-oriented men who form the hulk of the population and who also make up the largest percentage of violent offenders.

References

1. Bensing, R.C. and Schroeder, O. Homicide in an Urban Community. Springfield, Ill.: C.C. Thomas, 1960.

2. Bohannan, P. (ed.) *African Homicide and Suicide.* Princeton: Princeton University Press, 1960.

3. Fleuhr-Lobban, C. An Analysis of Homicide in the Afro-Arab Sudan. 1972.

4. Gonzalez, C.F. "Victimologia." *Policia Cientifica* 3(10, 1965):19–23.

5. Mushanga, T. *Criminal Homicide in Uganda.* East Africa Literature Bureau, 1974.

6. Mushanga, T. *Profile of Criminal Homicide.* East Africa Literature Bureau, forthcoming.

7. Schafer, S. "The victim and his criminal," paper presented to the President's Commission on Law Enforcement and Administration of Justice, Washington, D.C., 1967.

8. Sutherland, E. and Cressey, D.R. *Criminology.* Philadelphia: Lippincott, 1970.

9. von Hentig, H. "Der modus operandi beim verwandtenmord." *Archiv fur Kriminologie* 139(5–6, 1967):131–143.

10. Wolfgang, M.E. *Patterns in Criminal Homicide.* New York: Wiley, 1958.

11. Wolfgang, M.E. *Studies in Homicide.* New York: Harper and Row, 1967.

11

Patterns of Violence in Scotland

R. Emerson Dobash and
Russell P. Dobash

Violence in the Family

In this century research reports have consistently indicated that it is in a marital setting that women are most likely to be involved in violence, and this is usually as victims not attackers. It is in the institution of the family that the patriarchal legacy persists through the continuation of the hierarchical relationship between men and women. Male authority is still, regardless of the so-called liberation of women, revered and protected by social institutions and reinforced and perpetuated through the socialization of children.

Research findings relating to interpersonal violence consistently establish the association between intimate relationships and homicides and assaults, but social scientists have been just as consistent in their failure to note the direction of these attacks. In order to establish the direction and recurring patterns of violence in the family it is necessary to tease out findings and implications from existing research reports, and when this task is carried out it clearly indicates that it is women in their position as wives who are the most likely victims of systematic and persistent violent attacks in the family.

Homicides

MacDonald's early research on homicide in several countries revealed that men were much more likely to commit murder than women[17] and when women were killed they were predominantly the victims of attacks by intimates. In England and Wales between 1885–1905, of the 487 murders committed by men nearly a quarter of their victims (127) were their wives; another substantial proportion (115) were mistresses or 'sweethearts'.[14] Von Hentig's research on homicide in Germany provided consistent evidence of the relationship between marriage and violence directed at women. Of all the women killed by an intimate in Germany during 1931 61.5 percent were killed

Adapted with permission from Visage Press. Abridged version of R.E. Dobash and R.P. Dobash, "Wives: The 'appropriate' victims of marital violence." *Victimology,* 2(3/4):432–441, 1977–78. © Visage Press. All rights reserved. This research was supported from 1974–77 by a grant from the Scottish Home and Health Department.

by their husbands. The closer the attachment between a man and a woman the greater the risk to the woman of violent attack, ". . . when a woman is killed, (look) for her relatives, mainly the husband and after that her paramour.[23]

Wolfgang's research in Philadelphia provides additional support for this pattern in North America.[25] He substantiates the association between close, intimate relationships and violence that was discussed most explicitly by Simmel.[18] Using police records, Wolfgang found that primary relationships were involved in the majority of the murders he investigated. Again, female victims of murder were more likely to be killed by their spouse while male victims were more likely to be killed by someone outside the family.[24] Forty one percent of all female victims were killed by their husbands, only 10 percent of male victims were killed by their wives. The investigations of murder in England and Wales conducted by Gibson and Klein[10] and by Gibson[9] reveal that, for females, "Wives (including common-law wives) were usually . . . the most frequent victims of murder."[10]

Not only were female victims likely to be married to their attacker, they were also much more likely to have experienced very violent deaths. Defining severe violence as consisting of more than five acts of physical attack, Wolfgang concludes, "Husbands killed their wives violently in significantly greater proportion than did wives who killed their husbands."[25] Voss and Hepburn [24] found that females are much more likely to be beaten to death than are males. Women were also much more likely to be slain by a close friend or member of the family. Of the slayings involving non-whites 68.7 percent of the women were killed by a member of the family or close friend, and in the slayings involving whites, 78.9 percent of the women were murdered by friends or family members.[24] Other reports also reveal that the home is a violent setting,[1,21,5,16] but researchers have often failed to note that this violence is not randomly distributed among family members but is disproportionately directed at females. The homicide statistics outlined above provide an explicit verification of the differential use of violence between males and females. However, some research reports do not indicate a great divergence between the number of homicides committed by men and women,[17] but we would suggest that the explanations of the homicides committed by men and women are quite different. For example, Boudouris concludes that the high rates of homicides among non-white females in Detroit could be explained as a ". . . result of the women's act of self-preservation when attacked by a non-white male usually her spouse."[2] Wolfgang's work also points to this pattern, that husbands who were victims of homicide were a great deal more likely to have attacked their wives prior to their demise than were wives who were victims.[25]

The major implications to be drawn from research relating to homicides between men and women is that men are much more likely to commit homicides than women, and female victims are usually married to their attacker.

Women become a great deal more susceptible to physical attacks as the intensity of their relationship with men increases, and this pattern is even stronger when one examines research reports relating to assaults.

Assaults

Research conducted in England and Wales reveals that in 1950 and 1960 "domestic disputes" occurring in the home accounted for over 30 percent of all violent offences and 90 percent of these attacks were directed at wives by their husbands.[15] Boudouris[2] discovered that over 52 percent of a sample of assault cases in Detroit involved family relations. Unfortunately, Boudouris' work provides very little indication of the direction of this violence. Gelles' recent work reveals that violence was much more likely to be used by husbands than wives, and that nearly a quarter of the husbands attacked their wives on a regular basis.[8]

The work of Chester and Streather[4] though primarily concerned with the general pattern of divorce complaints in a county in Southern England uncovered a great deal about the direction of violence between adults in the family. They discovered that ninety percent of the 1500 divorce complaints examined involved reports of women complaining about violence from their husbands, and the vast majority of these women reported that they were subjected to "repeated violence" during the marriage.[4] In contrast to the work of Chester and Streather who analyzed divorce petitions in Britain, O'Brien [18] interviewed individuals seeking a divorce in the United States. Of the 150 individuals interviewed 28 spontaneously mentioned physical violence and this violence was primarily directed at women. Levinger's research on divorce revealed that physical abuse was one of the most commonly mentioned reasons for divorce and wives complained eleven times more frequently of violence than did husbands.[12] Indeed, we would be very surprised if this was not the case. Whitehurst, reporting patterns similar to those described by O'Brien and Levinger, indicates that physical force is a technique for maintaining and attempting to regain control in the family and males being "heavily socialized in instrumental and aggressive ways"[12,18] are much more likely to utilize force than women.[11,22] A recent extrapolation from divorce research in England estimates that 70 percent "of wives who petition for divorce each year . . . suffer from serious brutality."[7]

The research relating to violence occurring within the home points in an unequivocal manner to the differential nature of this violence. Men are usually violent toward their wives (common-law or legal) and this violence is often of a persistent nature. As Lystad recently concluded after an exhaustive review of the literature in this area, "The occurrence of adult violence in the home usually involves males as aggressors toward females."[13] Men are more likely to be taught to be aggressive and dominant, to be sensitive to affronts to their authority and attempt to preserve such authority and dominance through the use of force. They are more likely to be taught the skills related to physical force and to be inculcated with the willingness to use them in circumstances which "warrant" their use. One of these circumstances is systematically structured within the family in which women are to be subordinate to their husbands.

Social scientists have primarily conceptualized violence as a breakdown in social order in which either individuals or social structures are thought to be deviant or aberrant. We prefer to see violence used by men against women in the family as attempts to establish or maintain a patriarchal social order. Violence is used by men to chastise their wives for real or perceived transgressions of his authority and as attempts to reaffirm and maintain a hierarchical and moral order within the family. This conception of violence against wives is irrefutable in the light of the evidence sketched above and takes us beyond the sociological reductionism that permeates most of the work relating to interpersonal violence; research which is primarily oriented to determining the background characteristics of offenders and/or victims. We must go beyond the individuals or couples involved in violent marriages and episodes and seek explanations that are firmly embedded in a wider socio-historical context. We must also be less abstract about our conceptions of this form of violence. To conceive of violence in the family as 'marital violence', 'family violence' or even 'spousal violence' ignores the obvious fact that several types of violence occur in the family; husbands attack wives, children are assaulted by fathers or mothers, children attack each other and attack their parents, and wives use force against husbands. Even this degree of delimitation may not be enough since violence may mean anything from a slap to severe beatings resulting in death. The point is, we must be more concrete about our conceptions of violence, partialling out various types and forms of violence, not assuming a necessary interrelatedness between these forms and types and seeking explanations and understanding of these concrete forms in the wider society, as well as within family interaction.

Patterns of Violence in Scotland

We employed this methodology in our study of violence against women in Scotland. The results of a systematic analysis of police and court records and of in-depth interviews with women who have been beaten by their husbands[a]

---

[a]A fuller description of the techniques used in interviewing and a discussion of the issues concerning the representativeness of the sample of respondents and the police data appear in Dobash and Dobash (forthcoming).

reveals that the incidence of wife beating is quite high and that it is firmly associated with the domination, control and chastisement of women in their position as wives.

Police and Court Records

We analyzed 33,724 police charges which were processed through the courts of Edinburgh and one court district of Glasgow during 1974.[b] Because of the numerous problems inherent in the use of police and court reports,[3] we employed a technique which allowed us to go beyond the official charge and overcome the problem of uncritically equating the official charge with the nature of the event. All cases, despite the official charge, were read in order to ascertain if any physical violence was involved. All of the cases involving violence were then scrutinized more thoroughly in order to determine various aspects of the event, the sex of the offender and victim, and the nature of their relationship. When this examination was completed we found that violence was involved in only 11 percent of the cases (41 percent were traffic offences, 48 percent were non-violent breaches of the peace, theft and miscellaneous). A closer examination of the 3,020 cases involving violence reveals some rather extraordinary patterns. The violent offences were divided by sex of offender and victim into those which occurred between family members and those occurring between unrelated individuals. Only two of these categories contained 64.9 percent of all of the violent offences. Violence between unrelated males constituted the largest category (38.7 percent) and the second most frequent offence was violence by husbands directed at their wives (26 percent).

Table 11-1 provides a breakdown of the sex of offenders and victims. Almost all of the violent offenders reported to the police were males (91.4 percent) while a mere 8.6 percent of the offenders were females. In 1283 cases (44.6 percent) the victims were females while males were victims in 1589 cases (55.3 percent). Though men and women are almost equally likely to be victims they are not equally likely to be aggressors. Men are disproportionately represented as offenders.

Table 11-2 includes the distribution of the sex of the victims and offenders for all cases of violence occurring between family members. This included

---

[b]Edinburgh and Glasgow are cities of very different socio-economic complexions. Edinburgh is a city of approximately half a million people, the centre of the Scottish Civil Service, the cultural and historical capital of Scotland. Glasgow, a city of over one million people is a product of industrialism. As one of the birthplaces of the industrial revolution it suffers from the withering away of heavy industry. A city with a particularly working-class character, it has a high unemployment rate and poor housing that is only gradually being replaced. The particular district in which we examined police records was rather mixed in its socio-economic composition, since it included a large working-class estate as well as the University and its accompanying middle-class residences.

Table 11-1
Sex of Victim and Offender in All Cases Involving Violence

| | Victim | | |
Offender	Male	Female	Total
Male	1489	1136	2625
	(51.8)	(39.5)	(91.4)
Female	100	147	247
	(3.5)	(5.1)	(8.6)
Total	1589	1283	2872*
	(55.3)	(44.6)	(100)

*Sex unknown = 148.

Table 11-2
Sex of Victim and Offender in Violent Cases between All Family Members

| | Victim | | |
Offender	Male	Female	Total
Male	32	841	873
	(3.6)	(93.9)	(97.4)
Female	18	5	23
	(2.0)	(0.5)	(2.6)
Total	50	846	898*
	(5.6)	(94.4)	(100)

*Sex unknown = 148.

all assaults on spouses, children, siblings and parents. These data reveal that violence occurring between family members almost always involved male offenders and female victims, a pattern which prevailed in almost 94 percent of the cases. In every type of relationship, marital, parental, or sibling, the assaults followed the same pattern; males attacking females. In only 2.6 percent of the cases was the female the offender, but she was the victim in nearly 95 percent of the cases. Rarely were males assaulted in the home and even then it was more likely to be at the hands of another male member of the household. The home is simply not a dangerous setting for men, but it is for women. Females, whether they be sisters, mothers, wives or daughters, are more likely to be subject to control through the use of physical force than are their male counterparts—and it is in their capacity as wives that the risk is the highest and the danger the greatest.

The data in table 11-3 provide overwhelming support for this thesis. Husbands are only rarely assaulted by their wives (1.1 percent) whereas attacks on wives represent over 75 percent of all violence in the family setting. Women were very rarely assaulted by strangers on the streets, only 15 percent of the cases involving female victims occurred outside the family setting.

The data from our analysis of police and court records corroborates the findings of other research,[4,12,13,15,18] which indicate that women are much more likely to be the victims of violence which occurs between spouses.

The data presented here represent only a proportion of all the violence which occurs in the family. In the case of women, the rate of underreporting is very high and reflects feelings of shame, fear of retribution, negative experiences with past reportings, and the lack of viable alternatives available to them. Methodologically this presents a problem to which there is no real solution since no sampling procedure or data collection technique, no matter how sophisticated, well developed or anonymous will glean information about the incidence of violence unless the respondent is willing to make public (even if only on an anonymous questionnaire) what they consider to be secret and unshareable. In fact, evidence from our interview sample revealed that even among women who eventually did make their troubles public, only two out of every 98 assaults were reported to the police.[6]

We may well imagine that there is an equally high rate of underreporting of violence between all family members. It is unlikely, however, given the overwhelming body of evidence presented herein, that the proportion and direction of the violence between husbands and wives would be significantly altered even if we had complete information. Evidence from the interviews with bat-

Table 11-3
Type of Assaults Occurring between Family Members

	N	%
Wife assault	791	75.8
Husband assault	12	1.1
Child assault	112	10.7
Parent assault	73	7.0
Sibling assault	50	4.8
Mutual assault	6	0.6
Total	1044	100.0

tered women enables us to go beyond the issues of reporting and distribution and to capture some of the dynamics of the relationship in which women are assaulted.

Interviews with Battered Wives

In-depth interviews were conducted with 109 women who had been systematically and violently beaten on numerous occasions by their husband or paramour. These interviews lasted from two to six hours and covered a wide variety of topics from the childhood of the man and woman through the early stages of courtship and family life. Both the violent and nonviolent aspects of their relationship were examined in terms of factors associated with the emergence of violence and its continuation.

The early stages of the couple's relationship were not unlike those of any couple going out together. Most of the couples saw each other quite frequently and went out to movies, dancing and pubs several times a week. Once the relationship became somewhat serious both the men and the women began to restrict their activities with their same sex friends in order to spend more time together. Although more women were likely to restrict their social lives completely to their partner (61 percent), there was nevertheless a large percentage of men (41 percent) who did the same. During this period most of the men were very attentive and the women felt loved and satisfied with the relationship.

As the relationship continued there was a growing sense of exclusivity and possession. As would be expected, this was especially true among the males who were less likely to give up the 'nights out with the boys' but were more likely to expect that their girlfriend would go out exclusively with them. The man's increasing possessiveness and periodic displays of sexual jealousy served as signs of commitment to the relationship. Although, in retrospect, many of the women saw these as early warning signs, the behaviour was not uncharacteristic for courting couples and did not cause concern at the time. Some of the men did hit their future wives prior to marriage. Those who did (23 percent), usually did so because of sexual jealousy, usually unfounded, or as a protest against the women's threats to terminate the relationship. An analysis of these few cases indicates that the men came to consider it their right to question their future wife's activities and object through the use of physical force.

For most couples, however, violence did not occur until after they were married, but it usually occurred very soon after marriage. Fifty nine percent of the women had experienced violence by the end of their first year of marriage, and 92 percent within the first five years. After marriage, the authority relationships between men and women become more explicit. Husbands came to feel that their wives should meet their demands immediately and without question no matter how reasonable or unreasonable. The major sources of contention centered on what might be called 'wifely obligations' and the husband's authority. The obligations of a wife to care for her husband, to serve his needs and remain his exclusive sexual partner are all expectations which are supported to some degree by most social institutions and have very heavy moral overtones. In western society, a man feels that marriage gives him the right to expect domestic service and sexual exclusivity from his wife. The fulfillment of these behaviours is not only personally pleasant for him; it also becomes an outward sign of his 'rightful' possession of her, authority over her and ability to control her.

In our research, it was the real or perceived challenges to the man's possession, authority and control which most often resulted in the use of violence. A late meal, an unironed shirt, a conversation with any man no matter how old or young all served as 'justifications' for beatings. Many of the precipitating factors were exceedingly innocuous and would appear inexplicable without an understanding of the context of authority, subordination and control in which they occurred.

The historical and contemporary documents presented in this article elucidate the legal, religious and cultural legacies which have supported a marital hierarchy, subordinated women in marriage and legalized violence against them. The husband's right to control his wife by force extended far beyond slaps and shoves and into systematic beatings and brutalizing which sometimes resulted in death. Although domestic chastisement of wives is no longer legal, most of the ideologies and social arrangements which formed the underpinnings of this violence still exist and are inextricably intertwined in our present legal, religious, political and economic practices. Wives may no longer be the legitimate victims of marital violence, but in social terms they are still the 'appropriate' victims. Thus, it would be truly ironic if in the current climate, some magical twist of egalitarian terminology were to be used to deny centuries of oppression and to further repress contemporary women by obscuring the undeniable fact that spousal violence is to all extents and purposes wife beating.

References

1. Bard, M. "The study and modification of intrafamilial violence," in *Control of Aggression and Violence: Cognitive and Psychological,* pp. 149–164. Edited by J.L. Singer. New York: Academic Press, 1971.

2. Boudouris, J. "Homicide and the family." *Journal of Marriage and the Family* 33 (November, 1971):667–676.

3. Box, S. *Deviance, Reality and Society.* London: Holt, 1971.

4. Chester, R. and Streather, J. "Cruelty in English divorce: Some empirical findings." *Journal of Marriage and the Family* 34 (November, 1972): 706–712.

5. Curtis, L. *Criminal Violence: National Patterns and Behavior.* Lexington, Mass.: Lexington Books, 1974.

6. Dobash, R., Wilson, M., and Cavanagh, C. "Violence against wives: The legislation of the 1960's and the policies of indifference," paper presented at the National Deviancy Conference meeting, 1977.

7. Elston, E., Fuller, J., and Murch, M. "Battered wives: The problems of violence in marriages experienced by a group of petitioners in undefined divorce cases." Unpublished paper. Department of Social Work, University of Bristol, 1976.

8. Gelles, R.J. *The Violent Home: A Study of Physical Aggression Between Husbands and Wives.* Beverly Hills: Sage, 1974.

9. Gibson, E. *Homicide in England and Wales 1967-1971. Home Office Research Study No. 31.* London: Her Majesty's Stationary Office, 1975.

10. Gibson, E. and Klein, S. *Murder 1957 to 1968. A Home Office Statistical Division Report on Murder in England and Wales.* London: Her Majesty's Stationary Office, 1969.

11. Goode, W.J. "Force and violence in the family." *Journal of Marriage and the Family* 33 (November, 1971):624–636.

12. Levinger, G. "Source of marital dissatisfaction among applicants for divorce." *American Journal of Orthopsychiatry* 36 (October, 1966):804–806.

13. Lystad, M.H. "Violence at home: A review of the literature." *American Journal of Orthopsychiatry* 45 (April, 1975):328–345.

14. MacDonald, A. "Death penalty and homicide." *American Journal of Sociology* 16 (July, 1911):88–116.

15. McClintock, F. *Crimes of Violence.* New York: St. Martins Press, 1963.

16. Martin, D. *Battered Wives.* San Francisco: Glide Publications, 1976.

17. Moran, R. "Criminal homicide: External restraint and subculture of violence." *Criminology* 8 (February, 1971):357–374.

18. O'Brien, J.E. "Violence in divorce prone families." *Journal of Marriage and the Family* 33 (November, 1971):692–698.

19. Pitman, D.J. and Handy, W. "Patterns in criminal aggravated assault." *Journal of Criminal Law, Criminology and Police Science* 55 (December, 1964):462–476.

20. Simmel, G. *Conflict and the Web of Group-Affiliations.* New York: Free Press, 1955.

21. Steinmetz, S.K. and Straus, M.A. "The family as a cradle of violence." *Society* 10 (Sept/Oct., 1973):54–56.

22. Straus, M.A. "Sexual inequality, cultural norms, and wife beating," in *Victims and Society,* pp. 54–70. Edited by E. Viano. Washington, D.C.: Visage Press, 1976.

23. Von Hentig, H. *The Criminal and His Victim.* New Haven: Yale University Press, 1948.

24. Voss, H.L. and Hepburn, J.R. "Patterns in criminal homicide in Chicago." *Journal of Criminal Law, Criminology and Police Science* 59 (December, 1968):499–508.

25. Wolfgang, M. *Patterns of Criminal Homicide.* Philadelphia: University of Pennsylvania Press, 1958.

**Part IV
Summing Up**

Summing Up

Richard J. Gelles and
Claire Pedrick Cornell

Despite the many limitations and drawbacks to the research on family violence around the world, there are some areas in which we can draw conclusions.

First, family violence is certainly not confined to the United States, nor, for that matter, is it confined to families in developed, Western, industrialized nations.

Second, there is considerable variation from country to country in the likelihood of families being violent. The accumulated evidence from both empirical studies and position papers is that child abuse and spouse abuse are probably most common in Western, industrialized, developed nations. Developing countries also seem to have problems of abuse and violence, but these are interpreted as being grounded in the social disorganization caused by modernization and the resultant changes in family, clan, tribal, and social institutions. China is frequently described as a society with little or no problem with child or wife abuse, as are the Scandinavian countries.

Given the variation in extent of family violence around the world, it is quite possible that rates of family violence in the United States are *not* the highest in the world.

Explanations for the variation in family violence from culture to culture emphasize cultural differences in attitudes toward, and value placed on, children and the cultural appropriateness of using violence as a means of punishing perceived deviant behavior. Such cultural explanations are rarely empirically tested or examined, and seem to take the form of post hoc explanations for the absence or presence of family violence in particular cultures.

It is difficult, at present, to go much beyond these conclusions. Although it may be tempting to point out the similarities in factors related to family violence around the world, one must consider that these similarities can arise because researchers in other countries rely on their reading of the extensive literature on family violence in the United States to frame both their thinking and their research. The influence of U.S. research on other studies of family violence is apparent when investigators apply incidence rates from the United States to European countries, or when assumptions about family violence in other countries are based on the results of research in the United States.

What we found to be lacking in our examination of the literature on family violence around the world are cross–cultural studies of family violence. With few exceptions, nearly all the research we reviewed dealt with family violence in a single country. Given the methodological and definitional variations we discussed in this book, it is nearly impossible to directly compare the results of a child-abuse study in one country with research in a second or third country.

It is often highly unlikely that the investigators used the same nominal and operational definitions of violence and abuse.

What we need then is a knowledge of family violence built on cross–cultural research using precise and replicable definitions, measures, and research designs. Even more than this, we need cross–cultural research on family violence which empirically examines the factors that many investigators believe cause variation in the extent and patterns of family violence. Truly useful cross–cultural research on family violence should investigate social–structural variations, family–structural variations, and variations in cultural meanings and norms concerning children and family life.

Index

About the Contributors

Amiya Kumar Bhattacharyya is professor, head of the Department of Nutritional and Metabolic Diseases, and deputy director of the School of Tropical Medicine in Calcutta. He has been engaged in research on pediatric malnutrition at the school since 1957. As the only participant from the Third World to the Second International Congress on Child Abuse and Neglect in 1978, Dr. Bhattacharyya drew worldwide attention to nutritional child abuse. He has continued to write and speak on this subject.

Alison A. Davis has been a registered nurse at Sydney's Montrose Child Life Protection and Family Crisis Service since 1978, where she developed the role of a community pediatric nurse. This work includes clinical assessment of children in residence at the unit, matters related to Children's Court hearings, and education in child protection for the hospital schools of nursing and community health centers.

Rebecca Emerson Dobash received the Ph.D. from Washington State University and is now on the faculty of the University of Stirling in Scotland. She is currently a consultant for the British Department of the Environment and has also been a consultant for the U.S. Department of Health, Education and Welfare. Dr. Dobash was involved in a Social Science Research Council French-English exchange focusing on violence toward women. Since 1974 she has worked closely with the National Women's Aid Federation in England and Wales and the Scottish Women's Aid Federation. She has coauthored numerous papers on domestic violence.

Russell P. Dobash received the Ph.D. from Washington State University and now teaches at the University of Stirling. He is currently a consultant for the British Department of the Environment and has also been a consultant for the U.S. Department of Health, Education and Welfare. He was involved in a Social Science Research Council French–English exchange focusing on violence against women. Since 1974 he has worked closely with the National Women's Aid Federation in England and Wales and the Scottish Women's Aid Federation. He has coauthored numerous papers on domestic violence.

J.J. Gayford is a consultant psychiatrist, consultant to the Regional Alcoholic Unit, and psychiatric tutor at Warlingham Park Hospital in Surrey. He is also an Honorary Senior Lecturer at St. George's Hospital in London. He has published a number of papers on marital violence.

Ruth Hanson received the B.A. from Leeds University and has worked as a senior research associate and principal psychiatrist on the Birmingham Child Abuse Study at Queen Elizabeth Hospital, University of Birmingham. She has tested battered children and their parents, assisted in designing research instruments, scored test results, and written extensively. She has also worked as a research analyst in a delinquency study. Her areas of interest include deviance and educational psychology.

Sheila B. Kamerman is professor of social policy and social planning and co-director of cross-national studies of social service and family policy at Columbia University School of Social Work. She has been a consultant to several foundations and agencies in the United States and abroad on family policy, family support systems, women and employment, child welfare and child care. She is chairman of the National Academy of Science/National Research Council Panel on Work, Family and Community. Her recent books include *Parenting in an Unresponsive Society: Managing Work and Family Life* (1980), *Maternity Benefits and Leaves: An International Review* (1980) and *Helping America's Families* (1982).

David Levinson received the Ph.D. in anthropology from the State University of New York at Buffalo. He is now senior associate in research at the Human Relations Area Files in New Haven, Connecticut. Dr. Levinson is the author of numerous journal articles, the senior author of *Toward Explaining Human Culture* (1981), and the editor of *A Guide to Social Theory: Worldwide Cross-Cultural Tests* (1977).

Tibamanya mwene Mushanga was educated at Makerere University and the University of Wisconsin at Madison. He has taught at the University of Nairobi since 1973. He is the author of *Criminal Homicide in Uganda* (1974), *Crime and Deviance* (1976), and *Profile of Criminal Homicide* (forthcoming). In 1975 he attended the Fifth Congress of Crime Prevention and Treatment of Offenders as a United Nations consultant.

Eli H. Newberger received the M.D. from Yale University and the M.S. in epidemiology from the Harvard School of Public Health. He is now assistant professor of pediatrics at Harvard Medical School and lecturer on maternal and child health at the Harvard School of Public Health. Dr. Newberger is the founder of one of the first interdisciplinary child-abuse consultation units in the United States, at the Children's Hospital Medical Center in Boston. As director of the Family Development Study since 1972, he has worked to develop an adequate classification system and theory base for clinical practice and prevention of childhood illnesses of social and familial origin.

Kim Oates is a pediatrician with a particular interest in child development, mental handicap, and child abuse. He received his training at the Royal Alexandra Hospital for Children in Sydney, St. Mary's Hospital in London, and the Children's Hospital Medical Center in Boston. He practices at the Royal Alexandra Hospital for Children where he is the director of Medical Services and was formerly the head of the Department of Medicine and the head of the Child Development Unit. Dr. Oates is a member of the Executive Council of Defence for Children, is on the Executive Council of the International Society for the Prevention of Child Abuse and Neglect, and has recently edited *Child Abuse—A Community Concern.*

Michael G. Ryan trained at the Royal Alexandra Hospital for Children in Sydney. He spent a year as Fellow in the Child Development Unit at that hospital and during 1977 worked as a physician at the Odyssey House Adolescent Unit in New Hampshire. Since 1980 he has been the Regional Pediatrician at the Riverina Child Development Unit at Wagga Wagga in New South Wales. His special interests are emotional, physical, and intellectual handicaps in children and child abuse.

Selwyn M. Smith is currently professor of psychiatry at the School of Medicine, Faculty of Health Science, University of Ottawa. He is also psychiatrist-in-chief at the Royal Ottawa Hospital. Dr. Smith received the MBBS in medicine and surgery from Sydney University. He completed his postgraduate training in psychiatry in Birmingham, England. He was director of the Department of Forensic Medicine from 1975 to 1978 at the Royal Ottawa Hospital.

Dr. Smith is author of *The Battered Child Syndrome* (1975) and editor of *The Maltreatment of Children* (1978). He has also written many articles and chapters on child maltreatment.

Murray A. Straus has been a professor of sociology at the University of New Hampshire since 1968. He received the Ph.D. in sociology from the University of Wisconsin. Dr. Straus is a past president of the National Council on Family Relations. His books include *Behind Closed Doors: Violence in the American Family* (1980), *Social Causes of Husband-Wife Violence* (1980) and *Family Measurement Techniques* (1978).

Lesli Taylor is a graduate of Johns Hopkins Medical School and is currently a general surgical resident at Beth Israel Hospital in Boston. She plans a career in pediatric surgery with emphasis on trauma and inflicted injury.

About the Editors

Richard J. Gelles is professor of sociology and anthropology at the University of Rhode Island and lecturer on pediatrics at the Harvard Medical School. He directs the Family Violence Research Program at the University of Rhode Island and has published extensively on the topics of child abuse, wife abuse, and family violence. He is the author of *The Violent Home* (1974) and *Family Violence* (1979), coauthor of *Behind Closed Doors: Violence in the American Family* (1980), and coeditor of *The Dark Side of the Family: Current Family Violence Research* (1982).

Claire Pedrick Cornell is a special instructor of sociology at the University of Rhode Island. She was formerly a research analyst with the Family Violence Research Program at the University of Rhode Island. Her research interests include child abuse, spouse abuse, adolescent violence, and abuse of the elderly.